by Theresa A. Morse

FUTURE À LA CARTE

NEVER IN THE KITCHEN WHEN COMPANY ARRIVES

THE BEST I EVER TASTED!

THE BEST I EVER TASTED!

The best
I ever tasted!

THERESA A. MORSE

+++

DOUBLEDAY & COMPANY, INC., GARDEN CITY, NEW YORK 1969

LIBRARY OF CONGRESS CATALOG CARD NUMBER 69–15154

PRINTED IN THE UNITED STATES OF AMERICA

FIRST EDITION

TO MIGGIE, WHO HAS SHARED AND
BRIGHTENED ALL MY DAYS, WITH LOVE

Contents

All recipes and menus in this book (unless otherwise indicated) are for 6.

Recipes for Items followed by a star (*) may be located by consulting the Index.

THE BEST I EVER TASTED!

HH IS FOR HAPPY HOSTESS

"Will you join us for dinner a week from Saturday?" can be gay, magical words to the listener or the voice of doom. If the former, we immediately conjure up pleasant prospects of a delightful evening and a relaxed hostess who will have gathered together congenial guests of varied interests, will artfully seat them at table, and will provide wonderful food that, seemingly, wings its way effortlessly to the table. Cheers for this paragon whose warm hospitality is an adventure in happy living.

Conversely, how reluctantly we hear the voice of the nervous hostess. We love her and her husband but we hate their dinner parties. She is the hostess who is forever fluttering in and out of the kitchen, wrecking the party as she goes and generating outsized guilt feelings as well. (Had we only stayed home, what a peaceful evening she might be having!) We also shy away from the too-efficient hostess who, although entirely in command of the situation, serves so much food and works so hard producing it that she has no time or energy with which to make guests comfortable and happy.

Try not to take on more than you can easily handle. This goes for both the number of guests and the menu at any given dinner party. Plan ahead, cook ahead as much as possible, and, above all, move at a tempo that is comfortable for you. Keep in mind that most people prefer simple delicious meals to elaborate rich ones and that relaxed charm on the part of the hostess can launch a dinner party far better than complicated, last-minute, hot hors d'oeuvres. This knowledge can provide hostess peace of mind that works on a party like yeast.

Avoid the obvious pitfalls. Even if your best friend says it's a cinch, try a new recipe on your family before serving it to company. Keep records of your menus and guests, thus avoiding the embarrassment of repetition, and certainly it is the better part of valor not to gamble on an unusual dish that is not universally popular. For sheer frustration, watching guests push food around on their plates with a notable lack of enthusiasm can't be beat.

Keep broadening your cooking base—it will prove a fascinating challenge. Search the newspapers and magazines for new recipes, coax or bribe your friends into parting with their treasures, read cookbooks, and sign up for gourmet cooking lessons whenever you get the chance. Watch the one and only Julia on television. Even if you never intend wrestling with a suckling pig you will always pick up valuable tips and techniques from her and have stimulating entertainment as well.

My yardstick for a new dish is simple. It must be lovely to look at, delicious to eat, easy to make, *and* adaptable to beforehand preparation.

"Beforehand preparation" goes beyond mere cooking. How soothing (second only to opening one's eyes the morning *after* a smashing dinner party) to awaken on *the* day cozily secure in the knowledge that every bit of marketing is done, supplies of all kinds are in hand, linen is checked (maybe even the table set), flowers arranged, and all preliminary steps (if not total ones in some cases) have been taken toward completing appetizers, vegetables, salad, and dessert. It just might not turn out to be such a tough day after all. Especially if you happen to have a built-in husband who is helpful, interested, efficient, reliable, and gifted in the drinks department, as opposed to one who cannot mix a drink, put up a card table, wipe a dish, or put the children to bed.

The menus and recipes that follow in this book have evolved during the past four years (with the exception of a few indispensable repeats) since my cookbook *Never in the Kitchen When Company Arrives* was published. Generous friends and talented chefs have contributed their share of new dishes, and each fall I return to the London Cordon Bleu Cookery School where Miss Hume and Miss Downes, the two talented heads, demonstrate new and delectable dishes each season.

My proving ground has been the tiny summer inn that my husband and I operate on Martha's Vineyard, where we can accommodate twelve live-in guests at a time, although, come evening, we burgeon to about thirty diners. Thus for the summer months there is a large dinner party every night, and through our guests we have learned much about what is guaranteed to evoke raves in practically everyone. Remarks like "That's the best I ever tasted" or "When are you going to serve that spinach-mushroom dish again?" or "I never knew that lamb could be so delicious" clue us in and earn stars for the items. Conversely, our Mary is dependably alert for anything half-eaten on returning plates, and such a dish is either improved or banished forever.

Except for the summer months when our inn is in operation, I am a hostess, serving friends and family without benefit of help (other than the best of all possible built-in husbands), determined to enjoy my guests, be with them, and at the same time serve hot, delicious food. The recipes in this book are designed to make all this possible.

Entertaining can be frantic or fun. You, the hostess, can make or break the party. You are the heroine of the night, the show is entirely yours, and the final curtain can easily come down on deafening, warming applause. As any hostess will testify—there is no lovelier sound.

1.

APPETIZERS ARE CONTROVERSIAL

+++

Appetizers pose more problems than the entire dinner to follow. They are deemed elegant or superfluous, delicious or overwhelming, guaranteed to whet appetites or destroy them. They will initiate a meal or ruin it, should be in large variety or small—there are no hard and fast rules to guide the hostess. They can also be an outsized nuisance for the hostess who does EVERYTHING.

Londoners deal with this problem in a way to induce hostess envy across the ocean. Invariably the food accompanying pre-dinner cocktails is simple, requiring the minimum of attention from the hostess. Such ungourmet items as cheese sticks, tiny crackers, or salted nuts are conveniently at hand although seldom passed, the implication being that if you are foolish enough to be attracted by anything so appetite-destroying, do help yourself. The time allotted for drinking is usually a scant half hour, but wine is almost always served with dinner.

At the other end of the pole is an American hostess famous for her hors d'oeuvres, which are always too hearty, too irresistible, and too altogether wonderful. Guests, struggling with temptation and crashing down in defeat, invariably moan, "this should be the entire meal." So one night she did a little experimenting. Hearty, delicious, hot and cold hors d'oeuvres were served at a leisurely tempo throughout an extended drinking hour and were followed by an elegant dessert and coffee. Guests had been alerted and for once could eat appetizers to their hearts' content without fretting about either ruined appetites or avoirdupois. Sensational success!

For the conventional dinner party, my preference is for a relatively short drinking time (about half an hour) and the simplest and lightest of accompanying appetizers. While not so Spartan as my English friends, nevertheless when I have prepared what I fervently hope will be a splendid dinner, I hate to stand by and watch it being ruined by hungry guests gorging on appetizers.

So we come back to the fact that this is indeed a hostess decision. She knows her own preferences, presumably those of her guests, and, besides, she is in the driver's seat. Hence the appetizers that follow are for those who favor the few or the many, the light or the hearty. They share in common the great charm of requiring little or no last-minute attention. For convenience I am grouping those requiring a few minutes in the oven last.

STUFFED MUSHROOMS

18 uniform medium-
   sized mushrooms
¼ cup Roquefort cheese
¼ cup Camembert
   cheese
¼ cup ground walnuts

½ teaspoon
   Worcestershire sauce
½–1 teaspoon curry
   powder
Watercress or parsley

Remove stems from mushrooms. Cream together the Roquefort and Camembert. Add walnuts, Worcestershire sauce, and curry powder. Blend well and fill caps with the mixture. Decorate with watercress or parsley.

STUFFED CUCUMBER OR CELERY BOATS

3 *long slender cucumbers*
    OR
White inner stalks of
  2 bunches of celery
½ *pound cream cheese*
  at room temperature

1 *tablespoon grated*
  onion
2–3 *tablespoons red*
  caviar
2 *tablespoons fresh-*
  chopped parsley

Peel cucumbers, slice off ends, and cut in two, lengthwise. Scoop out seeds with a small spoon. (Or wash and dry celery.) Mix together cheese, onion, caviar, and parsley. Stuff cucumbers (or celery) with mixture and cut into bite-sized pieces. Decorate platter with parsley, celery tops, or watercress, and refrigerate until ready to serve.

TOMATO CANAPES

Butter at room
  temperature
16 *rounds white bread*
4 *tomatoes cut into*
  16 slices
Salt and fresh-ground
  pepper

½ *cup mayonnaise**
1–2 *teaspoons curry*
  powder
Fresh-chopped parsley

Butter bread rounds and place one slice of tomato on each. Season with salt and pepper. Blend together mayonnaise and curry powder and spread over tomato. Sprinkle with parsley. (If using homemade mayonnaise, make it with lemon juice instead of vinegar. If using commercial mayonnaise, add fresh lemon juice to taste.)

CHICKEN LIVER MOUSSE

½ pound chicken livers
¼ cup light cream
1 egg lightly beaten
Salt and fresh-ground
   pepper
Few drops Worcestershire
   sauce
1 small onion minced
   and sautéed
1 hard-cooked egg

Soak livers in salt water. Dry thoroughly and put through food mill. Add cream, egg, salt, pepper, Worcestershire sauce, and sautéed onion. Place in buttered ovenproof mold, set mold in a pan of hot water, and bake in 350-degree oven until set (about 45 minutes). Cool, turn out on a platter, garnish with grated hard-cooked egg, and surround with crisp crackers.

ROASTED POTATO SKINS

3–4 baking potatoes
Butter at room
   temperature
Salt and fresh-ground
   pepper
Brown paper

Bake potatoes in preheated 500-degree oven until done (30–40 minutes). Remove insides (these can be used for whipped potatoes) and cut skins into long even strips. Butter strips and season with salt and pepper. Place on brown paper and bake in 400-degree oven until crisp.

CAVIAR AND EGG CANAPES

Butter at room
  temperature
12 bread rounds lightly
  toasted on both sides
6 tablespoons caviar
  (black, if possible)

3 hard-cooked eggs
6 tablespoons sour
  cream
1 tablespoon minced
  onion
Fresh-chopped parsley

Lightly butter toast rounds and spread with caviar. Separate egg yolks and whites, grate the yolks, and chop the whites. In a bowl mix together yolks, whites, sour cream, and onion. Spread mixture over the caviar and sprinkle lightly with parsley.

CURRIED LOBSTER CANAPES

18 bread rounds 1½
  inches in diameter
1 teaspoon fresh
  lemon juice
1 cup coarsely chopped
  lobster meat

½ cup mayonnaise*
½–1 teaspoon curry
  powder
Paprika

Prepare bread rounds. Sprinkle lemon juice over lobster meat. Blend together mayonnaise and curry powder. Spread bread rounds lightly with some of curried mayonnaise. Cover with lobster and spread with balance of mayonnaise. Sprinkle lightly with paprika.

ARTICHOKE HEARTS AND SHRIMP

1 15-ounce can artichoke hearts

25 medium-sized cooked shrimp

1 egg yolk

¾ cup olive oil

¼ cup wine vinegar

2 tablespoons Dijon or Düsseldorf mustard

2 tablespoons fresh-chopped parsley

2 tablespoons chopped chives

1 tablespoon minced shallots or green onions

Salt and fresh-ground pepper

Cut artichokes and shrimp into bite-sized pieces. Place egg yolk in a mixing bowl and add oil, vinegar, and mustard. Beat well. Add parsley, chives, and shallots and mix well. Add artichokes and shrimp and gently turn in marinade. Season with salt and pepper. Marinate in refrigerator for at least 2 hours, turning occasionally. Serve in a shallow bowl with minimum of marinade so that artichokes and shrimp can be eaten with toothpicks or put on plain crackers (such as saltines, diet thins, etc.).

CHEESE DABS

1 jar cheese and bacon spread

¾ cup all-purpose flour

4 tablespoons butter at room temperature

Blend all the ingredients and put in refrigerator in wax paper to chill (so that it isn't too soft to handle) for at least an hour. Roll into balls the size of marbles and put one inch apart on lightly buttered cookie sheet. Flatten balls with the back of a fork lightly dipped in flour. Bake 15–20 minutes in 375-degree oven. Mixture will keep for days in the refrigerator and indefinitely in the freezer.

CHEESE COCKTAIL BISCUITS

1 cup grated sharp
   Cheddar cheese
¼ pound butter at
   room temperature
1½ cups all-purpose
   flour

½ teaspoon salt
Dash cayenne pepper
½ teaspoon
   Worcestershire sauce
Large Virginia peanuts

Blend together cheese and butter. Sift together flour, salt, and cayenne pepper. Blend into cheese mixture. Add Worcestershire sauce. Put in refrigerator to chill (as in previous recipe). Form into similar balls, insert a peanut in the center of each ball, but *do not flatten*. Bake on ungreased baking sheet at 375 degrees 12–25 minutes.

CRAB-STUFFED MUSHROOMS

18 uniform medium-
   sized mushrooms
4 tablespoons butter
1 small Bermuda onion
   finely chopped
1¼ tablespoons
   all-purpose flour
¾ cup crabmeat

2 tablespoons sherry
1½ tablespoons
   chopped parsley
Salt and fresh-ground
   pepper
¼ cup cornflake crumbs
1 tablespoon butter

Trim the stems from mushrooms and place, cap side down, on a well-buttered cookie sheet. Chop stems fine and reserve. Melt butter and sauté onion until golden. Add chopped mushroom stems to pan and cook for 5 minutes. Stir in flour and blend well. Add crabmeat, sherry, and parsley. Season to taste with salt and pepper. Stuff mushroom caps with the filling, sprinkle the tops with cornflake crumbs, and dot each with a little butter. Bake in 350-degree oven for 20 minutes.

TOASTED CHUTNEY AND PEANUT BUTTER

½ cup chutney
½ cup smooth
  peanut butter

18 white bread rounds
Small strips uncooked
  bacon

Chop chutney and mix with peanut butter. Toast bread rounds lightly on both sides and spread with mixture. Top with small strips of bacon. Put in 400-degree oven on a cookie sheet for 5 minutes or until bacon has cooked.

RED ONION PIZZAS

1 cup mayonnaise*
3 tablespoons
  Parmesan cheese

Party rye
Thin slices red onion

Mix together mayonnaise and cheese. Spread lightly (as though buttering) on party rye. Cover each piece with a thin slice of red onion. Heap about ½ teaspoon more of mayonnaise mixture on top of onion. Sprinkle with a little additional Parmesan cheese. (This much can be done ahead and pan kept in refrigerator.) When ready to serve, put in 450-degree oven for 10 minutes (or until brown).

CREAM CHEESE AND ANCHOVY

8 ounces cream cheese   Butter at room
Anchovy paste   temperature
1 loaf unsliced white
  bread

Blend together cream cheese and anchovy paste to taste. Remove crust from bread. Lightly butter end of loaf and spread with mixture. Cut off this end into a thin slice and repeat by spreading new surface with mixture and slicing thin until loaf is gone. Put on cookie sheet and toast under broiler until lightly browned on both sides.

PUFFED CHEESE ROUNDS

12 bread rounds   1 egg yolk
Butter at room   1 egg white
  temperature   Dash of Worcestershire
1 cup grated sharp   sauce
  Cheddar cheese
1 teaspoon baking
  powder

Toast bread rounds on one side. Turn and butter untoasted side. In a bowl mix together Cheddar and baking powder. Add egg yolk lightly beaten and then stiffly beaten egg white. Add

Worcestershire sauce and spread mixture on buttered rounds, mounding high in the center. Put under broiler until melted, puffy, and lightly browned.

BAKED ARTICHOKE HEARTS

1 15-ounce can artichoke
   hearts
Melba rye or white
   rounds
¼ pound butter, melted
Salt and fresh-ground
   pepper

¼ teaspoon garlic
   powder (optional)
Slivered almonds or
   sesame seeds

Drain artichokes and cut in half with kitchen shears. Place each half, cut side up, on Melba round. Arrange on a shallow ovenproof dish. In a small pan melt the butter, add salt, pepper, and garlic powder, and spoon generously into artichoke crevices, allowing some to run over on the rounds. Sprinkle with slivered almonds or sesame seeds. (This much can be done in the morning.) Bake in 350-degree oven for 10 minutes. Just before serving run under hot broiler for 2–3 minutes.

2.

FIRST COURSES ARE OPTIONAL

++

A first course is a festive way to launch a dinner party. There are many choices—it can be elaborate or simple, hot or cold, soup or salad, or you can skip it entirely. If cooking is easy for you or if the party is a special one and you want to make the effort, nothing could be nicer than an attractive first course. If, however, you prefer omitting it, then include a small unusual salad with your main course and that's fine, too. Again the choice is yours and should be determined by what is best for you.

STUFFED AVOCADOS

1 8-ounce package
   cream cheese
1–2 teaspoons cream
6–8 pitted ripe olives
   coarsely chopped
Fresh-chopped chives

Anchovy paste (to
   taste)
3 firm ripe avocados
Juice 1 lemon
Salad greens
Tart French dressing*
Chopped parsley

Soften cream cheese with cream. Add olives, chives, and anchovy paste. Cut avocades in half, remove stones, and peel. Fill the cavity of each with cream cheese mixture. Press the avocado halves together and brush outside with lemon juice. Wrap the three avocados in wax paper and chill in refrigerator. When ready to serve, toss salad greens (washed and dried) in French dressing. Make a bed of lettuce on individual plates. Cut avocados in thick, crosswise slices and put two slices on each salad. Sprinkle with parsley.

EGG IN TOMATO MAYONNAISE

6 hard-cooked eggs,
   shelled
⅓ cup mayonnaise*
⅓ cup commercial
   sour cream
1 ripe tomato, peeled,
   seeded, and finely
   chopped
1 teaspoon finely
   chopped tarragon
   leaves or ½ teaspoon
   dried

1 teaspoon lemon juice
Salt and fresh-ground
   pepper to taste
Salad greens, including
   Bibb, if possible
Tart French dressing*
Fresh-chopped parsley

Cut eggs in half lengthwise, put on a platter, cut side down, cover with Saran wrap, and refrigerate until ready to use. In a bowl combine mayonnaise, sour cream, tomato, tarragon, lemon juice, salt, and pepper. Cover bowl and refrigerate next to eggs. Wash and dry salad greens, store in bag or cloth in the refrigerator. When ready to serve, toss salad greens, lightly salted, in French dressing and arrange on individual plates. Arrange two egg halves, cut side down, on each bed of lettuce, spoon over mayonnaise-tomato dressing, and sprinkle each salad with parsley.

LOBSTER WITH BRANDY

Meat from 2 small
  boiled lobsters
½ cup mayonnaise*
1 tablespoon ketchup
2 teaspoons lemon
  juice
1 teaspoon chopped
  parsley
2 teaspoons finely
  chopped chives

2 tablespoons brandy
Salt and fresh-ground
  pepper
Salad greens
French dressing 4*
2 large tomatoes, each
  cut into 3 slices
Capers

Cut lobster meat into thin slices. In a large bowl blend together mayonnaise, ketchup, lemon juice, parsley, chives, and brandy. Add lobster meat, toss gently, and season to taste with salt and pepper. Chill in refrigerator. When ready to serve toss salad greens in French dressing and make individual beds of lettuce on salad plates. Put tomato slices in bowl with any remaining French dressing. Season with salt and pepper and arrange one slice in center of each plate. Cover with lobster mixture and sprinkle over with capers.

CANTALOUPE AND SHRIMP SALAD

2 large ripe cantaloupes
½ pound cold cooked shrimp

SALAD DRESSING

1 cup heavy cream	Dash paprika
3 tablespoons ketchup	Salt and fresh-ground
3 tablespoons lemon	pepper
juice	Chopped parsley

Peel cantaloupes, cut in two, remove seeds, and cut into balls with melon cutter. Blend together cream, ketchup, lemon juice, and paprika. Season to taste with salt and pepper and stir with whisk until it thickens a little. Add melon balls and shrimp and toss gently. Spoon into glass serving dishes or stemmed glasses. Sprinkle with parsley. Chill until ready to serve.

ASPARAGUS SALAD WITH CAPER DRESSING

18 stalks fresh	½ teaspoon fresh-ground
asparagus	pepper
⅓ cup red wine	⅔ cup olive oil
vinegar	Salad greens
1 tablespoon drained	1 tomato, concassed*
and chopped capers	Chopped parsley
1 teaspoon salt	

Cook asparagus until tender and "refresh"*. In a bowl combine vinegar, capers, salt, pepper, and olive oil. Beat until well blended and slightly thickened. Wash and dry salad greens, toss in a little of the dressing. Arrange cold asparagus on individual beds of lettuce and spoon over the dressing. Toss concassed tomato in bottom of salad bowl and scatter tomato, then parsley, over each plate.

ARTICHOKE HEARTS AND LOBSTER

1 egg yolk
½ cup olive oil
¼ cup wine vinegar
2 tablespoons Dijon
   or Düsseldorf
   mustard
2 tablespoons minced
   parsley
2 tablespoons chopped
   chives

1 tablespoon minced
   shallots or green
   onions
1 can small artichoke
   hearts
Lobster meat from
   2 small lobsters or
   1 large one
Bibb or Boston lettuce

Place egg yolk in bowl or blender and add oil, vinegar, and mustard. Beat well. If using blender, now pour into a bowl and add parsley, chives, and shallots. Mix with a large spoon. Drain artichoke hearts well, slice lobster meat into bite-sized pieces, and add to dressing. Marinate at least 2 hours in refrigerator, turning occasionally. Wash and dry lettuce. Arrange on individual plates, salt lightly, and pour contents of bowl over it.

MELON, CUCUMBER, TOMATO, AND AVOCADO

5 medium-sized
   tomatoes or 18
   cherry tomatoes if
   in season
2 long thin cucumbers
2 ripe cantaloupes
2 small ripe avocados

Salt
Fresh herbs (parsley,
   chives, tarragon, dill
   —as many kinds
   as possible)
Tart French dressing*

Scald and peel tomatoes. If using regular ones, cut each into six
wedges. Leave cherry tomatoes whole. Peel cucumbers, split
lengthwise into four, and cut into chunks. Peel melons, cut in
two, remove seeds, and scoop out balls with melon cutter. Cut
avocados into sections, making everything approximately the
same size. Put all the ingredients into a large bowl, season
with salt, and sprinkle with plenty of finely chopped herbs.
Shake French dressing hard and pour over liberally. Turn the
contents of bowl until all are lightly coated. Put bowl in
refrigerator for a few hours, turning occasionally. After a few
hours the amount of liquid will have increased. Serve with a
ladle into soup plates.

CAVIAR EGG MOUSSE

1 package unflavored
  gelatin
2 tablespoons lemon
  juice
2 tablespoons water
6 hard-cooked eggs
1 cup mayonnaise*
Salt and fresh-ground
  pepper
1 teaspoon
  Worcestershire sauce

4 ounces imported
  caviar
Dash onion powder
  (optional)
1–1½ teaspoons
  anchovy paste
Salad greens
French dressing 2*
2 small tomatoes cut
  into wedges
Chopped parsley

Dissolve gelatin in small bowl with lemon juice and water.
Place bowl over hot water and heat until gelatin is liquid. Rice
eggs in a bowl. In another bowl blend together mayonnaise,
salt, pepper, Worcestershire sauce, caviar, onion powder, and

anchovy paste. Add to eggs, mix lightly, and add gelatin. Grease six individual molds lightly with corn oil (or one large one, approximately 1½ pints) and fill with mixture. Chill in refrigerator at least 3 hours. Wash and dry salad greens and toss lightly in French dressing. Serve on individual salad plates or one big platter. Toss tomatoes in bottom of salad bowl. Season with salt and pepper. Unmold egg mixture on greens and add tomatoes to salad. Sprinkle with parsley.

STUFFED TOMATOES

6 medium-sized
   tomatoes
Salt and fresh-ground
   pepper
Powdered dill

6 canned artichoke
   hearts
Salad greens
French dressing 2*
Chopped parsley

SAUCE

1 cup mayonnaise*
½ cup commercial
   sour cream
1 teaspoon lemon
   juice

1 teaspoon grated
   onion
1 teaspoon curry
   powder

Peel tomatoes and cut off a wide enough slice from the top so that you can scoop out enough room for an artichoke. Line a plate with paper toweling and stand scooped-out tomatoes, upside down, on the toweling to drain for a few minutes. Turn upright and season *inside and out* with salt, pepper, and dill. Place an artichoke inside each tomato and refrigerate.

To make sauce—blend together in a bowl mayonnaise, sour cream, lemon juice, onion, and curry powder. Taste for seasoning. When ready to serve, toss salad greens lightly in French dressing and arrange bed of lettuce on individual plates. Put a stuffed tomato in the center of each and pour over mayonnaise dressing. Sprinkle with parsley.

EGG MAYONNAISE WITH TOMATOES AND CUCUMBERS

6 *hard-cooked eggs*
1 *cup mayonnaise**
½ *teaspoon finely chopped chives*
3 *long narrow cucumbers*
*French dressing 1**

4 *ripe tomatoes*
Salt and fresh-ground pepper
Iceberg lettuce
Finely chopped parsley or tarragon

Shell eggs and cut into even slices, using egg slicer. In a small bowl blend together mayonnaise and chives. Slice cucumbers, *unpeeled,* very thin, and marinate in a little French dressing. Cut tomatoes into chunks and marinate them in French dressing in a small bowl, and then season cucumbers and tomatoes with salt and pepper. Shred lettuce and refrigerate everything. When ready to assemble, toss lettuce lightly in French dressing and make a small bed on six individual plates. Arrange eggs overlapping in the middle of each and garnish with a ring of cucumbers and tomatoes. Spoon some of mayonnaise mixture over eggs and sprinkle salad with parsley or tarragon.

YOUNG SPINACH AND MUSHROOM SALAD

2 *pounds fresh*
tender young spinach
leaves
1 *pound medium-sized*
mushrooms

3 *strips bacon*
1 *tomato, concassed**
*Tart French dressing**

Wash spinach in several waters, remove stems, and use only the tender small leaves. Dry thoroughly in paper toweling and store in refrigerator. Cut off most of the stems and then slice mushrooms very thin. Cook bacon until very crisp and drain on paper towel. Concass the tomato. When ready to assemble, place spinach in salad bowl, sprinkle mushrooms over top, add well-shaken salad dressing, and toss gently until both spinach and mushrooms are well coated. Scatter tomato over the top and then sprinkle crumbled bacon over the entire bowl.

TOMATOES WITH AVOCADO DRESSING

1 *ripe avocado*
½ *cup mayonnaise**
1 *tablespoon lemon*
juice
1 *tablespoon onion*
juice
Dash Worcestershire
sauce

Salt and fresh-ground
pepper
4 *large ripe tomatoes*
Salad greens
Chopped chives or
parsley

Peel avocado and purée in blender, or push through a sieve. Add mayonnaise, lemon juice, onion juice, and Worcestershire sauce.

Season to taste with salt and pepper. Refrigerate until ready to use. Peel tomatoes and cut each into three thick slices. When ready to serve, arrange greens on individual plates, cover with two slices of tomato per plate, salt tomatoes lightly, and pour the avocado dressing over them. Sprinkle with chopped chives or parsley.

CUCUMBER SOUP

4 tablespoons chopped
  scallions or shallots
  or onions
2 tablespoons butter
2 long thin cucumbers
1 teaspoon wine
  vinegar
1 teaspoon fresh
  lemon juice
1 quart chicken stock*

½ teaspoon dried dill
  weed
3 tablespoons baby
  farina
Salt and white pepper
½ cup commercial
  sour cream
Chopped chives
Chopped parsley

Cook scallions in butter until soft. Add the cucumbers (peeled and cut into small chunks), vinegar, lemon juice, chicken broth, and dill. Bring to a boil, then add farina. Simmer, uncovered, for 30 minutes. Strain soup through food mill or sieve, pushing cucumbers through. Return soup to the pan and season to taste with salt and pepper. Before serving bring soup to just under a boil and beat in sour cream. Add chopped chives and parsley and serve. (The addition of a small dollop of sour cream to each soup bowl when serving adds to the appearance but is not necessary.) Very good cold.

ONION SOUP

5 large onions
3 tablespoons butter
1 tablespoon vegetable
   or olive oil
Salt
½ teaspoon sugar
1 tablespoon flour
3 pints beef bouillon

½ teaspoon Dijon
   mustard
Salt and fresh-ground
   pepper
6 bread rounds,
   toasted, or slices of
   French bread
Grated Parmesan cheese

Slice onions very thin. Heat butter and oil in a large heavy saucepan. Add onions and stir well to coat with butter. Cover the pan and cook over moderate heat for 20 minutes, stirring occasionally. Uncover the pan, raise heat, and sprinkle with a little salt and sugar. Cook for another 30 minutes or until onions have turned a deep rich brown. Reduce heat and stir in flour (with a little more butter, if necessary). Cook until butter is absorbed and flour slightly browned (2–3 minutes). Remove from heat long enough to slowly add *1 cup of bouillon*, and whisk well to blend. Return to heat, add balance of bouillon and mustard and simmer, covered, for 1 hour. Season to taste with salt and pepper. Serve with French bread and grated Parmesan. Or heap toasted buttered rounds with cheese, place in ovenproof soup tureen (or individual heatproof bowls) and pour soup over. Bake in 450-degree oven until cheese is bubbling (about 5 minutes).

BLENDER GAZPACHO

½ small onion sliced
1 clove garlic minced
1 small green pepper
   seeded and sliced
1 large cucumber
   peeled and coarsely
   chopped
3 ripe tomatoes peeled,
   seeded, and cut into
   wedges

Salt and fresh-ground
   pepper
½ teaspoon dried basil
2 tablespoons olive oil
6 cups strong chicken
   stock*
Chopped chives

Place all the ingredients except chives in blender and turn on lowest speed. Blend until well mixed but not smooth. Adjust seasoning. Can be served hot or cold. Just before serving sprinkle with chopped chives.

AVOCADO SOUP

3 ripe avocados
1–1½ teaspoons curry
   powder
Salt and fresh-ground
   pepper
1 cup heavy cream

1 quart chicken stock*
3 teaspoons lemon
   juice
Finely chopped chives
   or parsley

Peel avocados, cut in two, remove stones, and dice. In an electric blender blend together avocados, curry powder, salt, pepper, and cream. Heat together stock and lemon juice, add a little to avocado mixture, blend well, then turn contents of blender into remaining stock and simmer gently. Check seasoning and serve in soup tureen or individual dishes garnished with chopped chives or parsley.

CELERY VELOUTE

1 quart chicken stock*
1 small onion coarsely chopped
1 carrot sliced into ¼-inch pieces
3 stalks of celery cut into pieces
Salt and fresh-ground pepper

1 large egg yolk
2 teaspoons fresh lemon juice
Paper-thin lemon slices
Chopped parsley

Simmer broth and vegetables for 1 hour. Strain and season to taste with salt and pepper. In a bowl beat together egg yolk and lemon juice. Pour a little of the hot soup into this mixture and whisk well. Pour egg mixture into rest of soup and heat, stirring constantly and being careful not to let it come to a boil. Garnish with lemon slices and sprinkle with parsley.

QUICK LOBSTER AND CRAB BISQUE

1 can tomato soup
1 can pea soup
2 cans beef consommé
1 cup fresh crabmeat

1 cup sliced fresh lobster meat
3 tablespoons sherry
Chopped chives or parsley

Put all soups in blender and mix well. Pour into top of double boiler. Add crabmeat and lobster and heat thoroughly. Just before serving add sherry and chopped chives or parsley.

LEMON SOUP

3 eggs
¼ cup lemon juice
6 cups homemade
   chicken stock*

1 lemon sliced paper
   thin
Chopped parsley

In a bowl beat eggs until light and fluffy, then add lemon juice. Heat soup and stir about 2 cups of hot soup into egg mixture and whisk well. Pour this mixture into the balance of the hot soup and whisk until it begins to thicken. Serve in cups, garnish with lemon slices, and sprinkle parsley over the top of each cup.

QUICK SUMMER SOUP ✳ 1

1 large can V-8
   juice (1 quart, 14
   ounces)
½ cup sour cream
1–2 teaspoons onion
   juice

1 teaspoon
   Worcestershire sauce
Salt and fresh-ground
   pepper
Chopped chives

Blend together V-8 juice, sour cream, onion juice, and Worcestershire sauce. Season to taste with salt and pepper. Chill thoroughly. When ready to serve, ladle into cups and sprinkle with chives.

QUICK WINTER SOUP

1 can cream of
   tomato soup
1 can cream of
   asparagus soup
1 can cream of
   celery soup
1 can pea soup
2 cans chicken broth
2 teaspoons chopped
   chives

2 teaspoons chopped
   parsley
½ cup sherry (or dry
   vermouth)
Salt and fresh-ground
   pepper
Croutons

Blend together all soups and simmer for 30 minutes. Add chives, parsley, and wine. Season to taste with salt and pepper. Pour into soup tureen or individual soup bowls and scatter croutons over the top.

DINNER PARTY MENUS

✦✦✦

We come now to the meal itself. While I'm against hearty appetizers and only occasionally wish to burden myself with a first course, dinner is something else again. I want mine to be hot, easy to prepare, simple to serve, and altogether delicious. I keep records of what I serve because duplication is a disgrace and, given a choice, I'd rather eat mediocre food on hot plates than ambrosia on cold.

The menus that follow are designed with special emphasis on beforehand preparation. Everything cannot be ready before guests arrive, but if your dinner requires only that you return to the kitchen a few minutes before serving—well, by that time the party should be nicely under way and the guests won't feel you're a harried slave.

The success of those last few minutes in the kitchen hinges on preparedness. It presupposes that salad has been washed and dried, dressing mixed, odd jobs of preparing tomato wedges, sliced hard-cooked eggs, chopped parsley, fresh lemon juice, whipped cream, etc., have been gotten out of the way hours before. Those last few minutes are for assembling, correcting seasoning, checking that everything is hot and ready, and for making last-minute gravy or sauce if needed.

As it is your party, if the menus that follow seem scanty dinner-party fare, add hors d'oeuvres and/or a first course. There are those who favor one hearty appetizer (such as crab ravigote, baked mushrooms and shrimp, stuffed tomatoes, etc.) served on plates with forks and napkins while drinking in the living room. This is considered a substitute first course, but to my mind it is a nightmare. If you have no help, it is clumsy and difficult to manage. If you do have help, why not sit down comfortably and be served the first course at table?

With few exceptions, I have not included suggestions for rolls, bread, or toast, because I find that guests are inclined to resist that particular temptation, knowing there will be greater ones to come.

Before embarking on the menus to follow, a word about wine. If you enjoy wine, it is safe to assume that you have made a study of this fascinating subject from the masses of books, pamphlets, and vintage charts available. There are those who feel that cocktails should not precede wine at dinner and therefore eschew one or the other. There are those who feel that a festive meal is incomplete without wine and those who do not care for it at all.

Feeling that this is a personal matter, I am not offering any advice on the subject except to say that in cooking, use only good, healthy table wines and fine liqueurs. With a light hand, I might add—wine should enhance the flavor of a dish but not overpower it. If you don't happen to care for wine in your food, omit it wherever it appears. But if you do, then I can only say that inferior wine is to cooking what imitation vanilla is to baking. Both will spoil whatever they touch.

MENU 1

Entrée

LEG OF LAMB PATSY

MINT GRAVY

CHÂTEAU POTATOES

CARROTS WITH COGNAC

CUCUMBERS, GERMAN STYLE

Dessert

COFFEE SOUFFLÉ

COFFEE

LEG OF LAMB PATSY

Leg of lamb (about
   6 pounds)
Salt and fresh-ground
   pepper
½ teaspoon dry
   mustard
½ teaspoon ginger
   ½ teaspoon Ac'cent
Slivers of garlic
   (optional)

2 tablespoons cider
   vinegar
Flour
Paprika
¼ cup water
½ large onion, sliced
Celery tops
½ bottle mint sauce
Warm water
Bunch parsley or
   watercress

Wipe lamb with a damp cloth. Mix together salt, pepper, mustard, ginger, and Ac'cent. Insert slivers of garlic in tiny gashes in the lamb. Rub lamb well with mixed seasonings and sprinkle over with vinegar. Sprinkle lightly with flour and paprika. Let stand 4 hours at room temperature. Add water, onion, and celery tops to pan and put in preheated 400-degree oven for 20 minutes—then reduce to 350. Cook 30 minutes per pound, or less if pink lamb is preferred. Add a little more water from time to time if necessary. When about half done, remove some of the fat by tipping pan and spooning fat out, and pour over mint sauce. Baste well and continue basting occasionally until lamb is finished.

MINT GRAVY

To make mint gravy—remove lamb to a warm platter and take out onion and celery. Skim off more of the fat and heat roasting pan on top of stove. Add a little warm water and mint sauce and stir vigorously over heat until all particles from sides and bottom of pan are in the gravy. Correct seasoning, strain, and serve.

CHATEAU POTATOES

8 *medium-sized old potatoes*
4 *tablespoons butter*
Salt and fresh-ground pepper

Peel potatoes, cut into quarters lengthwise, and round sharp edges with vegetable parer or knife. Clarify butter. Heat heavy skillet, add clarified butter, and, when hot, add potatoes. Cook, uncovered, turning occasionally, until potatoes are browned. Turn into a cake pan. Cover and put into 350-degree oven with lamb for about 30 minutes.

To clarify butter—cut into pieces and place in saucepan over moderate heat. When butter has melted, strain into small bowl, thus eliminating the milky residue.

CARROTS WITH COGNAC

2 *bunches carrots*	½ *teaspoon salt*
¼ *pound butter*	2–3 *tablespoons cognac*
1 *teaspoon sugar*	*Chopped parsley*

Scrape carrots and cut into very thin slices (or shape into tiny bullets by rounding sharp edges of bite-sized pieces with vegetable parer). Melt butter in ovenproof dish, add carrots, and sprinkle with sugar, salt, and cognac. Cover dish and bake in 350-degree oven for 50–60 minutes, or until tender. Sprinkle with parsley before serving.

CUCUMBERS, GERMAN STYLE

3 *long thin cucumbers*	*Salt and fresh-ground*
½ *onion finely chopped*	*pepper*
3 *tablespoons olive oil*	*Chopped chives*
1 *tablespoon vinegar*	*Chopped parsley*

Wash cucumbers, slice thin, *unpeeled,* and put into ice water for at least 1 hour. Press liquid out between palms and put in bowl. Add onion, oil, vinegar, salt, and pepper and mix well. If dressing seems insufficient, repeat oil and vinegar in the same proportions and correct seasoning. Sprinkle with chives and parsley.

COFFEE SOUFFLE

2 tablespoons butter
¼ cup flour
1 cup milk
4 egg yolks well
   beaten

2–3 tablespoons
   powdered instant
   coffee
4 egg whites
½ cup sugar
½ cup coffee ice
   cream

Prepare six 6-ounce ovenproof ramekins by buttering them (with extra butter) and sprinkling bottom and sides with sugar. Shake out any excess. Preheat oven to 350 degrees. In a saucepan melt the 2 tablespoons butter over low heat. Stir in flour and whisk until bubbly. Add milk and continue to cook over moderate heat, stirring constantly, until mixture is very thick. Cool slightly, then beat in the egg yolks and powdered coffee.

Beat egg whites until they hold soft peaks. Beat in sugar gradually. When stiff, fold into egg yolk mixture. Set aside ½ cup of this soufflé mixture (to become part of sauce when serving finished dessert). Spoon remaining soufflé mixture into the prepared ramekins up to a half inch from the top. Bake for 35–40 minutes. Cool.

To serve—beat coffee ice cream to soften, and mix with reserved soufflé mixture. Guests can make a small incision in the top of the soufflé at the table and spoon sauce in.

MENU 2

Entrée

BAKED CHICKEN

BOULANGER POTATOES

PEAS (FRESH, FROZEN, OR SNOW)

MUSHROOM, CELERY, AND EGG SALAD

Dessert

CHOCOLATE FANTASY

COFFEE

BAKED CHICKEN

3 *large breasts of chicken split in two*	*Paprika*
OR	3 *tablespoons oil*
2 *2½-pound fryers cut into pieces*	3 *tablespoons butter*
	2 *cloves garlic minced*
Salt and fresh-ground pepper	½ *cup beef consommé*
	1 *cup sour cream*
Flour	*Chopped parsley*

Season chicken pieces with salt and pepper, and dredge lightly with flour on all sides. Sprinkle with paprika. Heat oil and butter in a large heavy skillet. When bubbling, add chicken, a few pieces at a time, and brown quickly. Remove to warm platter and continue until all pieces are browned. Add garlic and consommé to pan and stir well. Remove from heat and blend in sour cream. Return chicken to pan and baste well. Cover pan tightly and place in 350-degree oven for 40–50 minutes, or until tender. Place chicken on hot platter, spoon over some of gravy, and sprinkle with parsley. Serve balance in gravy boat.

BOULANGER POTATOES

8 medium-sized potatoes
3 medium-sized onions
Butter

Salt and fresh-ground
  pepper
1 bay leaf
2 cups beef consommé

Wash potatoes, peel, slice very thin, and dry well on paper towels. Slice onions, put into cold water, bring to a boil, and drain at once. Grease ovenproof dish with butter (or drippings if you have them on hand), and arrange potatoes and onions in layers, seasoning each layer with salt and pepper. Add bay leaf and fill dish three quarters full with consommé. Place in 350-degree oven 50–60 minutes, or until potatoes are cooked and well browned.

PEAS

2 pounds fresh peas
  (garden variety)
Salt and fresh-ground
  pepper

2 tablespoons butter,
  melted
1 tablespoon finely
  chopped mint

Cook peas in 1 cup boiling, salted water until tender, season with salt and pepper, and pour butter over them. Mix lightly and sprinkle with chopped mint.

Peas seem to have a special affinity for chicken and, given our choice, we take snow peas. They are seldom found fresh in the markets (except for Chinese grocery stores in the fall and early winter) but are very good frozen if not cooked for more than 2–3 minutes.

SNOW PEAS

3–4 tablespoons olive oil

2 tablespoons chopped onions

2 packages frozen snow peas (otherwise known as Chinese pea pods)

Salt

Heat oil in skillet, add chopped onions, and cook only until soft and transparent. Add frozen peas and mix well. Let cook for 2–3 minutes, stirring gently (they should be crisp, not soft). Season with salt and spoon into serving dish.

MUSHROOM, CELERY, AND EGG SALAD

¼ pound medium-sized mushrooms

4 white stalks celery

2 hard-cooked eggs

A few tiny celery leaves

2 pimientos finely chopped

Salt and fresh-ground pepper

French dressing 2*

Salad greens

Fresh herbs or dried (tarragon, dill, chives, etc.)

Chopped parsley

Trim mushroom stems halfway up and cut mushrooms in two. Cut celery into bite-sized pieces and hard-cooked eggs into chunks. Place mushrooms in a bowl, add celery, leaves, eggs, and pimientos. Season with salt and pepper. Pour French dressing over and toss gently. Let stand, covered, in the refrigerator until ready to serve. Wash and dry salad greens and store in refrigerator with wax paper package of chopped herbs and chopped parsley for garnish. To assemble salad, toss greens, lightly salted, in French dressing, add the herbs, and toss again. Serve on individual salad plates and pile mushroom mixture in center. Sprinkle with parsley.

CHOCOLATE FANTASY

5 egg whites
Pinch salt
1½ cups sugar
2 tablespoons dark
    cocoa
2–3 tablespoons brandy

1 cup heavy cream,
    whipped
1–2 tablespoons sugar
1 ounce semisweet
    or bitter chocolate

Preheat oven to 225 degrees. Beat egg whites and salt together until stiff but not dry. Mix together sugar and cocoa and add, gradually, to egg whites, beating until very thick. Add brandy to taste and pour into greased ring mold. Set in a pan of hot water is oven and bake for 1 hour. Remove from oven and let stand 10 minutes before turning out on serving platter.

Whip cream, sweeten to taste (can be done in the morning and stored, covered, in the refrigerator). Pile cream in center of ring. Sprinkle with chocolate, either grated or shaved with a vegetable parer.

MENU 3

Entrée

VEAL CHOPS MEDITERRANEAN
OVEN-CHIPPED POTATOES
YELLOW SQUASH FERGUSON
TOSSED GREEN SALAD

Dessert

BUTTERSCOTCH ICEBOX CAKE
COFFEE

VEAL CHOPS MEDITERRANEAN

6 thick loin veal chops
Salt and fresh-ground
 pepper
Flour
¼ cup oil
1 can beef bouillon
½ teaspoon lemon juice
2 teaspoons grated
 lemon rind
1 tablespoon
 Worcestershire sauce
½ cup pitted ripe olives
½ cup thinly sliced
 onions
¼ cup chopped
 pimientos
4 tablespoons capers
2 tablespoons butter
12 large mushroom caps
1 tablespoon ketchup
1 tablespoon sherry
Chopped parsley

Season chops with salt and pepper and dredge lightly with
flour. Heat oil in large heavy skillet and brown chops over

moderate heat on both sides until they are very dark. Add
bouillon, lemon juice, rind, Worcestershire sauce, olives, onions,
pimientos, and capers to the pan. Cover and simmer over low
heat for 45–60 minutes, or until tender. Heat butter and sauté
mushroom caps for 2–3 minutes. Add ketchup and sherry to
pan and blend well. Put chops on platter, spoon over strained
sauce from pan, and top each chop with two mushrooms.
Sprinkle with parsley.

OVEN-CHIPPED POTATOES

6 *long thin old potatoes*
¼ *pound butter, melted*
Salt

Scrub potatoes and cut, *unpeeled,* into thick slices. Soak slices
in ice water for at least 1 hour. Drain and dry thoroughly on
paper towels. Dip slices in melted butter and arrange them on a
large shallow baking dish. Bake the slices for 40–50 minutes
in a 375-degree oven, turning once or twice until they are crisp
and evenly browned. Season with salt and serve.

YELLOW SQUASH FERGUSON

6 *medium-sized yellow*
   squash
2 *tablespoons butter*
Salt and fresh-ground
   pepper

3–4 *tablespoons sour*
   cream
1–2 *tablespoons fresh-*
   chopped mint or
   ½ *teaspoon dried*
Chopped parsley

Cut squash into chunks, *unpeeled,* and cook in very little water
until tender, about 15–20 minutes. Turn into a strainer and

chop with a sharp knife so that water goes through strainer. Put into a double boiler. Add butter, salt, pepper, sour cream, and mint. Blend well. (This can be done in the morning.) Before serving, heat until piping hot, pour into a warm serving dish, and sprinkle with parsley.

TOSSED GREEN SALAD

Salad greens
2 sticks Belgian endive
1 long thin cucumber
½ red onion

3 tomatoes
Salt
French dressing 4*
Chopped parsley

Wash and thoroughly dry salad greens. Quarter endive. Peel and thinly slice cucumber and onion. Quarter tomatoes and put in separate bowl. Season with salt. Combine greens, endive, cucumber, and onion in salad bowl. Season lightly with salt and toss in French dressing. Spoon a little of the dressing over the tomatoes and arrange them over top of salad bowl and sprinkle with parsley.

BUTTERSCOTCH ICEBOX CAKE

2–3 packages ladyfingers
¼ pound sweet butter
2 cups confectioners'
   sugar
4 egg yolks lightly
   beaten
½ teaspoon vanilla

½ teaspoon powdered
   instant coffee
1 pint heavy cream,
   whipped
½ cup grated walnuts
   or pecans
½ cup ground
   butterscotch candy

Line bottom and sides of a small or medium-sized springform pan with ladyfingers. Cream butter, add sugar, and blend well. Add egg yolks, vanilla, and coffee, and beat 1 minute. Fold whipped cream into mixture and cover cake layer with one third of mixture. Sprinkle with nuts and butterscotch. Repeat twice, ending with nuts and butterscotch on top. Place in refrigerator for several hours or overnight.

MENU 4

Entrée

TOURNEDOS, SAUCE BÉARNAISE

BAKED BROILED POTATOES

SPINACH AND MUSHROOMS

ZUCCHINI SALAD

Dessert

MERINGUES FILLED WITH STRAWBERRIES AND PEACHES

COFFEE

TOURNEDOS, SAUCE BEARNAISE

Marinade (see below)
6 fillets of beef,
   7 ounces apiece
Salt and fresh-ground
   pepper

Butter
Sauce Béarnaise*
Chopped parsley

MARINADE

1 tablespoon vinegar
1 tablespoon
   Worcestershire sauce

5 tablespoons red
   wine
10 tablespoons oil

Put all ingredients for marinade together in bottle and shake well. Season fillets lightly with salt and pepper and marinate them, at room temperature, for 3–4 hours before cooking.

To cook—dry fillets thoroughly on paper towels. Heat heavy skillet, add butter, and, when foaming, add fillets (if necessary, use two pans but cook them all at the same time). Sauté fillets about 5 minutes per side and remove to hot platter or individual warmed plates. Season with a little more salt and spoon Béarnaise sauce over (kept warm in a small bowl standing in a bowl of hot water). Sprinkle with parsley and serve.

BAKED BROILED POTATOES

6 *baking potatoes*	*Onion juice (optional)*
1 *teaspoon butter*	¼–½ *cup heavy cream*
Salt and fresh-ground	*Parmesan cheese*
pepper	

Bake the potatoes for 1 hour. Cut in two, scoop out the potato (skins can be used for the appetizer roasted potato skins*), and put in bowl. Add butter, salt, pepper, and a little onion juice. With a fork mash lightly but avoid making potato too smooth. Place an 8-inch flan ring (or removable ring of small springform pan) on a flat cookie tin and fill ring with potato mixture. Dribble cream over mixture and let stand 10–15 minutes. Remove ring and bake in 375-degree oven for 20 minutes. Just before serving run under hot broiler to brown.

SPINACH AND MUSHROOMS

3 10-ounce packages
  frozen chopped
  spinach
1 pound medium-sized
  fresh mushrooms
Butter

1 can cream of
  mushroom soup
Salt and fresh-ground
  pepper
Garlic powder (optional)
Topping (see below)
Paprika

TOPPING

½ cup commercial sour cream
½ cup mayonnaise*
2 tablespoons fresh lemon juice

Cook spinach according to directions on package but only until entirely thawed (as there will be further cooking). Put into wooden bowl and chop a little finer. Remove stems from mushrooms, reserve sixteen whole caps, and chop all stems and remaining caps quite fine. Sauté mushroom caps in butter in one pan (they will be used for garnish) and sauté caps and mushroom mixture in another. Add sautéed mushrooms and mushroom soup to spinach, season with salt, pepper, and garlic powder. Spoon into ovenproof serving dish. Spread topping over surface. Arrange mushroom caps on topping and sprinkle lightly with paprika. Heat in a 375-degree oven for 20 minutes.

To prepare topping—combine ingredients, blend well, and heat slowly after spinach is prepared.

ZUCCHINI SALAD

4 medium-sized
  zucchini
¼ cup vinegar
1 teaspoon salt
1 teaspoon sugar
4 tablespoons minced
  green onion
3 tablespoons finely
  chopped green pepper

3 tablespoons sweet
  pickle relish
2 tablespoons chopped
  pimiento
2 tablespoons chopped
  parsley
½ cup salad oil
Salad greens
1 tomato, concassed*

Wash zucchini and cut into thin slices, *unpeeled.* Drop into
boiling, salted water and cook 2 minutes. Drain well and cool.
In a bowl or jar combine vinegar, salt, sugar, onion, pepper,
pickle relish, pimiento, parsley, and oil. Beat or shake hard.
Pour over cooled zucchini and store in refrigerator, *covered,* for
at least 2 hours. Stir gently occasionally. Wash and dry salad
greens and store in refrigerator with concassed tomato in wax
paper. To assemble salad, arrange greens on individual plates
and spoon zucchini over it. Sprinkle a little extra dressing on
the lettuce and scatter tomato over each plate.

MERINGUES FILLED WITH STRAWBERRIES AND PEACHES

2 *egg whites*
Dash salt
½ *cup superfine sugar*
½ *teaspoon vanilla*
Fresh or frozen
   strawberries and
   peaches

Kirsch or orange
   curaçao
½ *pint heavy cream,*
   whipped and slightly
   sweetened

Beat egg whites until frothy, add salt and beat until stiff and dry. Add sugar gradually and continue beating until very stiff. Add vanilla. Cover ungreased cookie sheet with heavy ungreased brown paper (if none on hand, cut up a large grocery bag) and form six meringue shells on to the brown paper. (See note at end of recipe.) Bake in 275-degree oven 45–60 minutes or until lightly browned and crisp to the touch. Crush the center. Stored in airtight tin until ready to use. Put fruit in a bowl (thawed, if using frozen fruit) and sprinkle with a little superfine sugar and liqueur to taste. Cover and store in refrigerator. When ready to serve, fill the meringue cases with fruit, spoon over whipped cream, and decorate with meringue mushrooms.

Note: An ordinary pastry bag plus a few metal tubes make piping meringues, whipped cream, icing, etc., for desserts easy, and the results are very attractive. Instructions come with a pastry set and it is fun to do. Star tips, rosette tips, twisted rope effects, a tube for writing—all are available and worth buying.

MENU 5

Entrée

SHERRIED CHICKEN
PIMIENTO POTATOES
BROCCOLI RING WITH MUSHROOMS
MIXED GREEN SALAD

Dessert

FRENCH PARTY CAKE
COFFEE

SHERRIED CHICKEN

¾ cup flour
2–3 teaspoons salt
Garlic powder
    (optional)

2 2½-pound fryers cut
    into serving pieces
        OR
3 large chicken breasts
    split in two
10 tablespoons butter

SAUCE

6 tablespoons butter
¾ cup dry sherry
3 tablespoons soy
    sauce

3 tablespoons fresh
    lemon juice
½ teaspoon ginger

Combine flour, salt, and garlic powder and lightly dredge pieces of chicken. Shake off excess flour. Melt butter in heavy skillet and brown chicken on all sides. Place in ovenproof baking dish.

To make sauce—in a saucepan melt butter and add sherry, soy sauce, lemon juice, and ginger. Bring to a boil, stirring constantly, and pour over chicken. Bake, uncovered, in 350-degree oven for 1 hour, or until tender. Baste occasionally and turn chicken once during baking.

PIMIENTO POTATOES

24 *tiny new potatoes*
   OR
6 *large potatoes*
Salt
¼ *pound butter*

2 *slices pimiento,*
   drained and chopped
1 *tablespoon fresh*
   lemon juice

Scrub new potatoes, or scrub and peel large ones and cut into potato balls. Let stand in cold water for at least 30 minutes. Cook in boiling salted water to cover for 12–15 minutes, or until soft. Drain potatoes, shake over burner for a minute or two to dry, then sprinkle with salt. Melt butter, add pimiento and lemon juice, and pour over potatoes. Toss gently. (This can be done in the top of a double boiler in the morning and left, covered, until evening, when potatoes can be reheated over boiling water.)

BROCCOLI RING WITH MUSHROOMS

2 *pounds fresh broccoli*
    OR
3 *boxes frozen spears*
2 *tablespoons butter*
2 *tablespoons flour*
1 *cup light cream*
4 *egg yolks*
Salt and fresh-ground
  pepper

4 *egg whites*
1 *pound mushrooms*
2 *tablespoons butter*
2 *tablespoons lemon*
  juice
1 *hard-cooked egg,*
  grated

Wash broccoli, discard coarse outer leaves and tough bottom of stalks, and soak for 30 minutes in cold salted water. Drain and split stalks lengthwise. Cook in boiling salted water to cover until tender, about 15 minutes. Refresh* and chop broccoli until quite well mashed. (If using frozen broccoli, cook according to directions on the box but subtract 2 minutes from cooking time.) Melt butter, remove from stove, and add flour. Blend well, return to heat, and bring to a boil. Slowly pour in cream, whisking steadily. Cook until thick, remove from heat, and add well-beaten egg yolks. Blend well and add broccoli. Season with salt and pepper. (This much can be done in the morning.) Before baking, beat egg whites, with a pinch of salt, until very stiff, and fold into broccoli mixture. Correct seasoning and pour into a buttered, lightly floured ring mold. Place in a pan of boiling water and bake in 350-degree oven 30–35 minutes.

Trim ends of stems of mushrooms and cut mushrooms in two. Sauté in butter, season with salt and pepper, and after 2–3 minutes add lemon juice. At the same time hard cook the egg, grate, and store in wax paper. Mushrooms can be done in the morning and left in skillet to reheat.

To serve—turn ring mold out on heated platter, fill center with mushrooms, and sprinkle grated egg over broccoli.

MIXED GREEN SALAD

Romaine lettuce	*Watercress*
Boston lettuce	*French dressing 3**
Belgian endive	*1 tomato, concassed**
Baby spinach leaves	*Chopped parsley*

Wash and dry greens. Toss in French dressing, add tomato for final toss, and garnish with parsley. Serve from bowl or arrange on individual salad plates.

FRENCH PARTY CAKE

⅓ cup flour	*1¼ cups cake flour*
4 large eggs	*sifted*
¾ cup sugar	*5 tablespoons tepid*
2 teaspoons vanilla	*melted butter*
Grated rind of 1 lemon	
or 1 orange	

Preheat oven to 325 degrees. Prepare an 8-inch by 8-inch cake pan by buttering bottom and sides, lining with wax paper cut to fit bottom exactly, and buttering wax paper. Shake flour over bottom and sides and knock out excess. Put eggs, sugar, vanilla, and rind into large mixer bowl. With an egg beater, or preferably an electric hand mixer, beat this mixture on the stove over *almost simmering* water (not touching bottom of pan) until mixture feels warm to the touch and has doubled in size (about 5–6 minutes.) Remove bowl to electric mixer, or beat by hand, until mixture is thick and mousselike (8–10 minutes). Sift one quarter of the sifted flour over top of mixture and, with a rubber spatula, quickly fold into batter. Add *a little* of the tepid butter and repeat, alternating flour and butter until both have been incorporated into the batter. (By adding butter slowly, it will blend instead of dropping to the bottom.) Pour into the prepared pan (two thirds full) and bake in lower middle level of the oven for 35–40 minutes (or until cake springs back when lightly touched). Let cool 10 minutes, then loosen sides with sharp knife, cover with cake rack (turned upside down), and turn cake out. Peel off wax paper lining and let cool. If not frosting at once, wrap in plastic bag and store in a tin. This can be made two days ahead and frosted on *the* day. It also freezes beautifully.

BUTTER CREAM ICING

3½ ounces superfine
   sugar
2½ ounces water
2 egg yolks
5 ounces sweet butter
   at room temperature

Flavoring (coffee,
   vanilla, chocolate,
   kirsch, curaçao,
   brandy–whatever
   preferred)
Shaved chocolate or
   chocolate sprinkles

Dissolve sugar in water and boil until liquid makes a short thread when poured off a spoon or stretched between finger and thumb. Take off heat at once. Cream egg yolks and pour sugar syrup over them in a steady stream, beating as you pour. Beat mixture until thick and mousselike (5–7 minutes). In another bowl cream butter until white and well whipped. Slowly beat the mousse into the whipped butter and beat until well blended. Add flavoring. (A great favorite is coffee flavoring —1 teaspoon of instant coffee—and after splitting cake and frosting bottom layer, add 1 ounce of melted bitter chocolate to balance of icing for the top layer.)

To ice—cut cake in two crosswise and sprinkle lightly with kirsch or curaçao (optional). Ice bottom layer and cover with top. Add melted chocolate to icing (as above) and frost top and sides, swirling top with spoon to create a pattern. Decorate with chocolate shavings. When serving, I suggest cutting cake in two and then cutting thin portions, across cut sides, as this dessert is elegant and rich.

MENU 6

Entrée

VEAL SCALOPPINE

NOODLES ALFREDO

GREEN BEANS AND BROWN BUTTER

ASPARAGUS SALAD WITH CAPER DRESSING

Dessert

STRAWBERRY SPONGECAKE

COFFEE

VEAL SCALOPPINE

½ *cup flour*
Salt and fresh-ground
   pepper
Onion salt
Paprika

12 *slices veal pounded*
   thin
4 *tablespoons oil*
2 *tablespoons butter*

SAUCE

1 *cup beef consommé*
1 *teaspoon*
   Worcestershire sauce
1 *teaspoon ketchup*
1 *tablespoon dry*
   wine, red or white
1 *tablespoon Italian*
   tomato paste

Garlic salt (optional)
Chopped chives
½ *pound fresh*
   mushrooms, sliced
Butter
Salt and fresh-ground
   pepper
Chopped parsley

(If butcher cuts veal very thin, it need not be pounded. Otherwise he will do it for you.) Put flour, salt, pepper, onion salt, and paprika in paper bag and shake a few slices of veal at a time. Heat some of the oil and butter (in the ratio of 2 oil to 1 butter), and when hot, add veal, a few pieces at a time, and brown well on both sides. Put aside and continue until all are done (adding more oil and butter when needed).

To prepare sauce—in a bowl mix consommé, Worcestershire sauce, ketchup, wine, tomato paste, garlic salt, and chives. Return meat to frying pan and pour mixture over it. Mix well, bring to a boil, then simmer, uncovered, for 20–25 minutes. In a separate pan sauté the sliced mushrooms in butter. Season with salt and pepper. Arrange meat in copper pan (or other shallow, ovenproof serving dish) and spoon over sauce from pan. Sprinkle sautéed mushrooms over the top. If not serving immediately, cover with aluminum foil and later reheat in 350-degree oven with noodles and beans. Just before serving, sprinkle with parsley.

NOODLES ALFREDO

1 pound broad noodles
       OR
1 pound green noodles
¼ pound butter

½ cup grated
   Parmesan cheese
1 cup heavy cream

Cook noodles in a large deep kettle containing 3–4 quarts rapidly boiling water to which 4 teaspoons salt have been added. Cook until barely tender (about 7 minutes) and drain well. While noodles are cooking, melt butter in a saucepan and stir in cheese and cream. Cook over very low heat, stirring constantly, until the cheese has melted and the sauce is smooth. When noodles are drained but still hot, pour sauce over them and toss well. Arrange in casserole or other ovenproof serving dish and, if necessary, keep hot, covered, in 350-degree oven. Serve with additional Parmesan cheese.

GREEN BEANS AND BROWN BUTTER

1½ pounds fresh green beans
     or
2 packages frozen whole beans
4 tablespoons butter

2 tablespoons lemon juice
Salt and fresh-ground pepper
Chopped parsley

If beans are fresh and young, wash well, snip off ends, and cook whole. If large, put beans on cutting board in neat bunches and cut in half. Cook in boiling, salted water 1 inch deep, covered, until tender (15–20 minutes). Refresh* and drain well. (If cooking frozen beans, follow instructions on box but cook 2 minutes less than prescribed time.) Melt butter and allow to brown. Add lemon juice, salt, and pepper. Pour over beans and toss lightly with two forks. Put in ovenproof serving dish and reheat in 350-degree oven, uncovered, for 10 minutes.

ASPARAGUS SALAD WITH CAPER DRESSING

24 stalks fresh asparagus
    OR
24 stalks canned green
   asparagus
Salt
Salad dressing
12 strips pimiento

Salad greens (Bibb,
   iceberg, Boston, etc.)
Fresh or dried herbs
   (tarragon, dill,
   chives, etc.)
Chopped parsley

SALAD DRESSING

⅓ cup red wine vinegar
⅔ cup olive oil
1 tablespoon drained
   and chopped capers

1 teaspoon salt
½ teaspoon fresh-ground
   pepper

Measure dressing into a jar with a screw-on top. Shake hard. If using fresh asparagus, stand it upright in cold water a half inch deep until ready to cook. Break off tough lower part of stalks and then scrape about 2 inches of remaining stalk. Wash well in cold water. Cook asparagus in a narrow deep pan in rapidly boiling salted water, uncovered, for 15–20 minutes, or until tender. Remove gently to colander and refresh*. Drain well, spread on a platter, season with salt, and spoon over 2–3 tablespoons well-shaken salad dressing. Cut pimientos in strips and store in small dish. Wash and dry salad greens. Snip herbs (except parsley) and wrap in wax paper. Chop parsley, keeping it separate, and store all ingredients in refrigerator.

To assemble salad—toss greens and herbs (except parsley)

in salad bowl with a little of the dressing. Arrange on individual plates, put four asparagus stalks on each plate, spoon over a little extra caper dressing, and sprinkle with parsley.

STRAWBERRY SPONGECAKE

¾ cup sifted all-purpose flour	4 eggs
	1 cup sugar
⅛ teaspoon salt	Pinch cinnamon

FILLING

1 quart fresh strawberries	Butter at room temperature
3–4 tablespoons superfine sugar	1 cup heavy cream, whipped
2–3 tablespoons sherry	

To prepare cake tins—cut out two rounds of wax paper to fit bottoms of two 8-inch cake tins. Rub bottom and sides of tins with softened butter (or salad oil), cover with wax paper, rub paper with butter, and sprinkle with superfine sugar and then flour. Shake out surplus sugar and flour.

To prepare cake—sift flour and salt together three times. Break eggs into a bowl, start beating, add sugar and cinnamon gradually, and beat together until thick and mousselike (about 10 minutes in a mixer). It is done when it makes a ribbon on itself. *Using a metal spoon,* cut and fold flour into mixture. Turn into prepared pans. Bake 25–30 minutes in a 375-degree oven (test with cake tester). When done, run a knife around edge of each pan, cover with a wire rack (upside down), and quickly turn right side up. Gently peel off paper lining. When cool, turn cakes up again.

To prepare filling–wash and hull strawberries. Reserve about twenty of the biggest and best to garnish top of cake. Sweeten them lightly with sugar. Slice remaining berries, sprinkle with sugar and 1–2 tablespoons sherry. Let stand for a few hours.

To assemble cake—lightly butter bottom layer and spread with sliced berries and juice. Cover with top layer, spread with whipped cream, and decorate with reserved berries.

MENU 7

Entrée

ROAST BEEF

DILLED NEW POTATOES

RATATOUILLE NIÇOISE

ARTICHOKE AND AVOCADO SALAD

Dessert

COFFEE TORTE VIENNESE

COFFEE

ROAST BEEF

*Standing rib roast
   (first three ribs)
Salt and fresh-ground
   pepper
Garlic powder
   (optional)*

*1 tablespoon
   Worcestershire sauce
½ cup chili sauce
1 tablespoon A-1 sauce*

Remove beef from refrigerator 3 hours before roasting. Wipe well with paper towel and sprinkle with salt, pepper, and garlic powder. Mix together Worcestershire sauce, chili sauce, and A-1 sauce and pour over meat. Place in 500-degree oven. After 45 minutes (15 minutes per rib) turn oven *off. Do not under any circumstances open the door.* The beef must remain in the closed oven for *a minimum of 2 hours* after the heat is turned off (regardless of size). If, after 2 hours, you are not quite ready to serve, turn on oven to 200 degrees so that meat will stay hot but will not cook further. The beef will be evenly rare, juices will be well distributed, and natural gravy plentiful.

DILLED NEW POTATOES

24 small new potatoes with red or brown skins
Salt and fresh-ground pepper

¼ pound butter, melted
Finely chopped fresh dill or dried dill
Chopped parsley

Scrub potatoes. With the end of a vegetable parer, scrape a narrow circle around the middle of each. Soak in cold water for 30 minutes. Cook in boiling salted water to cover about 15 minutes, or until tender. Remove from heat, drain, and shake over heat for a minute or two. Season with salt and pepper, pour melted butter over them, and add dill. Toss gently to coat potatoes with butter and dill. Pour into serving dish and sprinkle with parsley.

RATATOUILLE NICOISE

1 large onion
4 tablespoons oil
1 large eggplant
2 zucchini
2 tomatoes
        OR
Strained tomatoes from smallest can
1 clove garlic

4 tablespoons butter
2 tablespoons chopped parsley
1 small bay leaf
Salt and fresh-ground pepper
¼ cup grated Swiss or Cheddar cheese
Butter

Slice onion very thin and sauté slowly in 2 tablespoons of the oil in large heavy skillet. Peel and cube eggplant, wash and slice zucchini (if small—otherwise peel also), peel, quarter, and seed tomatoes, and crush garlic. When onion is soft and transparent, add remaining oil and butter to pan and when hot add eggplant, zucchini, tomatoes, garlic, parsley, and bay leaf. Season to taste with salt and pepper and cook, uncovered, over medium heat until tender, 20–25 minutes. (This much can be done in the morning.) When ready to serve—heat ratatouille in top of double boiler over boiling water. When hot, pour into buttered ovenproof serving dish, sprinkle with grated cheese, dot with butter, and run under broiler for a minute or two.

ARTICHOKE AND AVOCADO SALAD

1 15-ounce can artichoke
  hearts
*French dressing 2**
1 large ripe avocado

2–3 tablespoons fresh
  lemon juice
Salad greens
Chopped parsley

Drain and halve artichokes. Put in bowl and marinate with some of French dressing. Peel avocado, cut in half, remove stone, and cut into thin slices. Put in bowl, sprinkle with lemon juice, cover. Wash and dry salad greens and store with artichokes and avocado in refrigerator.

To assemble—toss greens in French dressing, make a bed of lettuce on six individual salad plates, and arrange artichokes and avocado on top. Sprinkle with parsley.

COFFEE TORTE VIENNESE

3 *eggs*   Pinch salt
½ cup superfine sugar   3 ounces sweet butter
¾ cup cake flour

FROSTING

3 egg yolks   ¾ cup water
⅓ cup sugar   ½ pound sweet butter
1 ounce cornstarch   at room temperature
Pinch salt
2 tablespoons espresso
   instant coffee

Grease 8-inch springform pan lightly with oil. Warm eggs in shells in hot water. Break eggs into mixer bowl, add sugar, and beat at high speed for 10 minutes (20 minutes if beating by hand). Sift flour and salt together and fold into mixture lightly. Melt butter, cool slightly, and pour over mixture. Fold in lightly. Pour into prepared springform pan and bake in 350-degree oven for about 30 minutes (test for doneness with cake tester). Cool for 5 minutes, place on rack and remove sides of springform. Cut across horizontally (to make 2 layers).

To prepare frosting—in a saucepan beat together egg yolks, sugar, cornstarch, and salt with a wooden spoon. Dissolve instant coffee in water and add to mixture. Bring mixture to a boil, whisking as it thickens. Cook until thick enough to spread. Cool partially and beat in sweet butter, a little at a time. Frost bottom layer, cover with top layer, and frost top and sides. Decorate by piping some design around the edge with balance of frosting, or sprinkle over torte shaved chocolate, toasted almonds—whatever happens to be at hand.

MENU 8

Entrée

LOBSTER IN CASSEROLE
TOAST POINTS
POTATO OMELET
SAUTÉED ARTICHOKE HEARTS
MIXED VEGETABLE SALAD

Dessert

STRAWBERRIES WITH RASPBERRY SAUCE
OLD-FASHIONED SUGAR COOKIES
COFFEE

LOBSTER IN CASSEROLE

½ *pound mushrooms sliced*
1 *cup sour cream*
2–3 *tablespoons fresh lemon juice*
3 *tablespoons chopped parsley*
3 *tablespoons chopped chives*

Salt and fresh-ground pepper
2 *pounds cooked lobster meat cut into bite-sized pieces*
3 *tablespoons herb butter (see below)*
Parmesan cheese
Paprika

HERB BUTTER

2 *ounces sweet butter*
1 *tablespoon chopped fresh herbs (tarragon, chives, dill, parsley, etc.)*
½ *teaspoon lemon juice*

Sauté mushrooms in sour cream, add lemon juice, parsley, and chives. Season with salt and pepper. Add lobster meat, blend lightly, add a little more sour cream if necessary. Pour into oven-proof baking dish, dot with herb butter, sprinkle with Parmesan cheese and paprika. Place in 400-degree oven for 10 minutes and then run under broiler for a minute or two. Serve with toast points.

To prepare herb butter—cream butter, add herbs and lemon juice and blend well. (This is very convenient to have on hand for broiled meat or fish, so suggest that you double or triple the recipe whenever you make it.)

To make toast points—remove crusts from sliced white bread and toast lightly on both sides, then cut in half into triangles. They do not need to be buttered and can be made ahead and kept on a plate, covered.

POTATO OMELET

3 *tablespoons bacon fat or oil*
2 *cups peeled, diced, raw potatoes*
Salt and fresh-ground pepper

In a heavy saucepan melt the fat and, when very hot, add potatoes. Stir well until potatoes are coated with fat. Reduce heat and cook until tender (about 30 minutes) when underside will be nicely browned. Add more fat occasionally, if needed. Fold over like an omelet and transfer to a warm ovenproof platter. Before serving, run under hot broiler for a few minutes.

SAUTEED ARTICHOKE HEARTS

2 15-ounce cans artichoke
  hearts
3 tablespoons butter
Salt and fresh-ground
  pepper

Garlic salt (optional)
2–3 tablespoons fresh
  lemon juice
Butter
Chopped parsley

Drain artichokes. Sauté in butter until lightly browned. Season with salt, pepper, and garlic salt and sprinkle with lemon juice. Turn into lightly buttered ovenproof dish, dot with a little extra butter, and run under broiler or into hot oven before serving. Sprinkle with parsley.

MIXED VEGETABLE SALAD

Mixed salad greens
1 can baby beets
1 can whole tiny
  green beans
Tart French dressing*
2 tomatoes

1 hard-cooked egg
Chopped chives
Salt and fresh-ground
  pepper
Chopped parsley

Wash and dry salad greens. (If fresh vegetables are available, so much the better.) Marinate beets and beans separately in French dressing. Peel and quarter tomatoes and add them to bowl with beans. Grate hard-cooked egg and put in wax paper. Store all ingredients near each other in the refrigerator.

To assemble—toss greens in French dressing with chives. Season lightly with salt and pepper. Make bed of lettuce on individual salad plates and arrange vegetables attractively. Season vegetables lightly, sprinkle with grated egg and parsley.

STRAWBERRIES WITH RASPBERRY SAUCE

*1 quart fresh
    strawberries
Superfine sugar
2 tablespoons orange
    curaçao or kirsch*

*1 10-ounce package
    frozen raspberries
1 tablespoon fresh
    lemon juice*

Wash and hull strawberries. Cut very large ones in two, leave smaller ones whole. Sprinkle with sugar and curaçao. Let stand 1 hour. Thaw raspberries until entirely soft, then put through food mill or sieve. Add lemon juice to strained raspberries and, if necessary, a little more sugar. Pour over strawberries and refrigerate. Let stand at room temperature for about 1 hour before serving.

OLD-FASHIONED SUGAR COOKIES

¼ *pound butter at*
  room temperature
1 *cup sugar*
1 *egg (or 2 yolks)*
  beaten
1 *tablespoon cream*
½ *teaspoon vanilla*
1½ *cups all-purpose*
  flour

¼ *teaspoon salt*
1 *teaspoon baking*
  powder
2 *tablespoons melted*
  butter
Confectioners' sugar

Cream butter. Beat in sugar and blend well. Add egg, cream, and vanilla. Sift together flour, salt, and baking powder. Fold into mixture. When dough is smooth, place on wax paper and wrap. Store in refrigerator for at least 1 hour before baking (dough will keep a week in the refrigerator and freezes well). When ready to bake, lightly butter cookie sheet. Make small balls about the size of walnuts and place 2 inches apart. With back of a fork lightly dipped into flour, flatten each cookie with a crisscross effect. Bake in 375-degree oven for 7–8 minutes and remove to wax paper. While still warm, brush lightly with melted butter. When cool, sift confectioners' sugar over cookies and store in an airtight cookie tin.

MENU 9

Entrée

ROAST DUCK
CHIVED WHIPPED POTATOES
GLAZED ONIONS AND CARROTS
APPLESAUCE

Dessert

CHOCOLATE AND COFFEE TART
COFFEE

ROAST DUCK

2 plump ducks
   (weighing 5–6 pounds
   apiece)
Giblets
1 lemon cut in two

1 clove garlic
Salt and fresh-ground
   pepper
Paprika
6–7 tart apples

GRAVY

Giblet broth
1–2 tablespoons
   cornstarch
¼ cup water
1 cup fresh orange
   juice

1–2 tablespoons
   orange curaçao
   (optional)
Finely chopped duck
   livers

Wash ducks inside and out and dry well with paper towels. Wash giblets and simmer, covered, in about 3 cups of water or stock for about an hour. Strain. Reserve duck livers and chop fine. Rub ducks with lemon halves, squeezing juice over them. Split clove of garlic and rub over skin. Season ducks inside and out with salt and pepper and sprinkle lavishly with paprika. Peel, core, and quarter apples and fill duck cavities with them. Place ducks, breast side up, on a rack in large roasting pan in a 350-degree oven. Do not baste, since ducks are fat. Prick several times during cooking and turn occasionally to brown evenly. Tip pan and spoon out melted fat a few times. Roast about 30 minutes per pound, but make sure ducks are cooked through and tender.

To make gravy—when ducks are brown and crisp, remove to warm platter. Pour off most of fat from pan, leaving about 2 tablespoons. Put over heat and slowly add giblet broth. Scrape sides and bottom of pan for all particles. Dissolve cornstarch in water and pour into pan. Stir well. Add orange juice and curaçao. Correct seasoning. Add chopped livers and pour into warmed gravy boat.

CHIVED WHIPPED POTATOES

8 *medium-sized old potatoes*	*Salt and fresh-ground pepper*
2 *tablespoons butter*	*Finely chopped chives, scallion tops, or minced onion*
2 *tablespoons cream*	

Scrub and peel potatoes. Cut in half and put in pan. Cover with cold water, bring to a boil, and cook, covered, until soft, about

20–25 minutes. Drain and shake over heat for a minute or two to dry. Put into a bowl (mixer preferably) and add butter, cream, salt, and pepper. Mash (or blend well with beater) until smooth. Add chives and correct seasoning. If made ahead, put in double boiler and, just before serving, reheat uncovered.

GLAZED ONIONS

18 small-to-medium   1 teaspoon sugar
   white onions   Paprika
3 tablespoons butter

Peel onions, put in pan, cover with cold water, and bring to a boil. Remove at once, drain well. In a heavy skillet melt butter, add sugar and onions. Sprinkle lightly with paprika and cook over very low flame, turning occasionally, until tender, browned, and glazed, about 30–40 minutes.

GLAZED CARROTS

2 bunches carrots   Salt
2 tablespoons butter   Chopped parsley
2 tablespoons sugar

Peel carrots with vegetable parer and cut into chunks about 1 inch long. Round cut edges with vegetable parer. Place in saucepan, cover with water, and add butter, sugar, and salt. Bring to a boil, reduce heat to medium, cover and cook for 15 minutes. Remove lid, turn heat up to high, and boil fast (thus reducing remaining liquid to a syrupy glaze). Shake the pan so that all the carrots will be coated, and for these last few minutes watch carefully to prevent burning. (Both vegetables can be cooked in the morning.) To serve, either mix carrots and onions together or serve in double ovenproof vegetable dish. Reheat in oven while making gravy for duck.

APPLESAUCE

(If you live in apple country, make yours from fresh apples. If not—commercial applesauce with a little treatment is very good.)

FRESH APPLESAUCE

6 tart cooking apples	1 tablespoon butter
3–4 tablespoons water	Dash salt
Rind ½ lemon thinly	½ teaspoon cinnamon
pared	½ teaspoon lemon
1 tablespoon sugar	juice

Wash and quarter apples but do not pare. Cook slowly, tightly covered, in water (just enough to keep apples from burning) and lemon rind. When soft and pulpy put through food mill or coarse strainer. Stir in sugar, butter, salt, cinnamon, and lemon juice. Taste and correct flavor.

CANNED APPLESAUCE

1 large jar applesauce	1 teaspoon cinnamon
1 tablespoon fresh	Sugar
lemon juice	

In a bowl blend together applesauce, lemon juice, and cinnamon. Taste and, if necessary, add a little sugar.

CHOCOLATE AND COFFEE TART

1 6-ounce package
    semisweet chocolate
    bits
¼ pound butter
2 cups Rice Krispies

1 quart coffee ice
    cream
Semisweet chocolate,
    shaved or grated

Melt chocolate bits in top of double boiler over hot water. Blend in the butter. Add Rice Krispies and stir until well coated with chocolate mixture. Butter a 9-inch pie plate and pour mixture in. Spread evenly over bottom and sides of dish to form a crust. Let stand at room temperature for several hours. When ready to serve, fill with coffee ice cream and sprinkle shaved chocolate over the top.

MENU 10

Entrée

BAKED STEAK CREOLE

BAKED STUFFED POTATOES

BEANS AND MUSHROOMS

MIXED GREEN SALAD AND MUSTARD DRESSING

Dessert

FRENCH CHOCOLATE CAKE

COFFEE

BAKED STEAK CREOLE

Sirloin steak 2½ inches
   thick
Salt and fresh-ground
   pepper
Garlic powder
   (optional)
1 cup ketchup

3 tablespoons
   Worcestershire sauce
1 tablespoon fresh
   lemon juice
¼ pound butter, melted
1 large Bermuda onion,
   sliced
1 green pepper, sliced

Wipe steak with paper towel and put in shallow roasting pan.
Season with salt, pepper, and garlic powder and brown quickly
under preheated broiler. Remove steak. Set oven heat at 350
degrees. Season unbroiled side of steak with salt, pepper, and
garlic. Mix together ketchup, Worcestershire sauce, lemon juice,
and melted butter. Pour over steak. Top with onion and pepper

slices and bake, uncovered, for about 45 minutes. (Test a little earlier if very rare steak preferred.) Remove to warm ovenproof platter, season lightly with a little additional salt, and keep warm in turned-off oven while making gravy. Put steak on the top of stove and heat contents. If very thick, add a little boiling water or consommé to pan and scrape sides and bottom. Pour sauce, unstrained, into warm gravy boat. Sprinkle parsley on steak and serve.

BAKED STUFFED POTATOES

6 medium-sized Idaho
   potatoes
2 tablespoons butter
2 tablespoons cream
Salt and fresh-ground
   pepper

1 tablespoon chopped
   chives
1 tablespoon chopped
   parsley
Paprika

Preheat oven to 375 degrees. Scrub potatoes with vegetable brush and dry well on paper towels. With a little softened butter, rub the skins of each and bake in a shallow pan or on oven rack for 1 hour, or until soft. Cut off top, scoop out potato into a bowl. Add butter, cream, salt, pepper, chives, and parsley. Blend well. Check for seasoning and refill shells. Dot with butter and sprinkle with paprika. When preparing to serve, reheat in oven with the steak for about 15–20 minutes.

BEANS AND MUSHROOMS

1½ pounds green beans   *1 tablespoon fresh lemon*
¾ pound mushrooms   *juice*
3 tablespoons butter   *Salt and fresh-ground*
                              pepper

Trim ends of beans and cook whole (or sliced in two) in a covered pan in boiling, salted water. Refresh*. Slice mushrooms and sauté in butter for 3–4 minutes. Add lemon juice and a little more butter. Mix well. Add the beans and blend long enough to heat thoroughly. Season with salt and pepper.

MIXED GREEN SALAD AND MUSTARD DRESSING

Salad greens
½ teaspoon dill weed
Fresh-chopped parsley

Mix together available salad greens (Bibb, Boston, iceberg lettuce, romaine, watercress, etc.) Add dill weed and parsley and toss in mustard dressing.

MUSTARD DRESSING

1 teaspoon Dijon mustard
1½ tablespoons olive oil
¼ teaspoon salt

¼ teaspoon fresh-ground
   pepper
4 tablespoons wine vinegar

Blend ingredients in a jar and shake well before using.

FRENCH CHOCOLATE CAKE

½ cup cocoa
¾ cup boiling water
¼ pound butter
2 cups sugar
1 teaspoon vanilla
½ teaspoon baking
   soda

½ cup sour cream
2 cups pastry flour
⅛ teaspoon salt
3 egg whites stiffly
   beaten

ICING

½ cup brown sugar
½ cup water
2 tablespoons butter
2 squares bitter
   chocolate

2 cups confectioners'
   sugar
Pinch of salt
1 teaspoon vanilla

Dissolve cocoa in water and cool. Cream together butter and
sugar. Add the cocoa, vanilla, and baking soda (mixed with the

sour cream). Sift flour and salt four times. Cut into the mixture with metal spoon until thoroughly absorbed. Fold in stiffly beaten egg whites. Pout into two 8-inch prepared cake tins (see Strawberry Spongecake*) and bake in a 350-degree oven for 20 minutes (or until done when tested with a cake tester). Cool before removing from pans. Run knife around edge, cover with wire racks (upside down) and turn over quickly. Peel off paper from cake bottoms. Spread icing between layers and over cake.

To prepare icing—in a saucepan bring brown sugar, water, and butter to a boil. In a separate pan melt chocolate and add to mixture. Add confectioners' sugar, whisk well, and add salt and vanilla. Beat until smooth and thick.

COMPANY FOR LUNCH

+++

Entertaining for lunch has special charms in that the meal is usually informal and guests prefer simple food and not too much of it. Planning ahead for this meal pays rich dividends, since it comes in the middle of the day when there is no pinch-hitting husband on the premises. Hence the menus that follow are designed to please guests and keep the hostess relaxed and happy with emphasis on day-before preparation.

MENU 1

Entrée

ASPARAGUS ROLLED IN HAM

MIXED GREEN SALAD

Dessert

BRANDIED PEACHES

GLAZED COOKIES

ASPARAGUS ROLLED IN HAM

2 cans mammoth   1¼ cups Hollandaise*
    green asparagus tips   4–5 cups cooked rice
2 tablespoons butter   Chopped parsley
6 slices boiled ham
    ⅛–¼ inch thick

Drain juice from asparagus cans into a large saucepan and heat. Add asparagus and let simmer gently for 5 minutes. Melt butter in skillet and sauté ham slices over medium heat (about 2 minutes to a side). Remove ham to breadboard, place three stalks of asparagus on each, and roll up. Store in ovenproof dish and heat in 350-degree oven before serving. Reheat rice in top of double boiler, uncovered. When read to serve, spoon rice on to a warm serving platter, arrange ham rolls on top, spoon Hollandaise over it, and sprinkle with parsley.

MIXED GREEN SALAD

Salad greens (2 or   4 white stalks celery
    3 kinds)   coarsely chopped
Garden herbs, fresh   1 hard-cooked egg
    or dried   coarsely chopped
1 green pepper   Tart French dressing*
    coarsely chopped   Salt and fresh-ground
½ red onion sliced   pepper
                             Chopped parsley

Wash and dry salad greens. Prepare herbs, green pepper, onion, celery, and egg and store with salad greens in wax paper in the refrigerator. When ready to serve, toss all ingredients except egg and parsley in the French dressing. Sprinkle top with egg, season lightly with salt and pepper, and sprinkle with parsley.

BRANDIED PEACHES

2 cans Elberta
    freestone peaches
    (1 pound, 14 ounces
    each)
4 tablespoons butter
    at room temperature
½ cup brown sugar

Pinch cinnamon
2–3 tablespoons brandy
2 tablespoons syrup
    from peaches
Sour cream
Cinnamon

Drain peaches well and place, cup side up, in a shallow baking dish. Combine, in a small bowl, butter, sugar, cinnamon, brandy, and peach syrup and blend well. Spoon about 1 teaspoonful into each peach cup. Bake in 350-degree oven for 30 minutes, basting occasionally. When cool, place a small dollop of sour cream in the center of each and sprinkle lightly with cinnamon.

GLAZED COOKIES

½ pound butter at
    room temperature
1 cup sugar
1 egg yolk

2 cups cake flour
    sifted three times
1 teaspoon cinnamon
1 egg white
1 cup broken walnuts

Cream together butter, sugar, and egg yolk. Add flour and cinnamon sifted together. Lightly butter two regulation cookie sheets and pat mixture very thin on the sheets. Beat egg white until frothy and brush over surface of the dough (this can be done with pastry brush or clean hands). Press coarsely chopped walnuts into dough lightly. Bake in 375-degree oven for 10–12 minutes. Cut immediately into squares or rectangles, as cookies quickly become crisp.

On the day before, make the Hollandaise sauce, cook rice, prepare the salad ingredients (including French dressing), and bake the cookies. On *the* day, reheat the Hollandaise over a pan of hot water (it need only be warm). At all times keep cookies or cake in an airtight tin where they will remain fresh for several days.

MENU 2

Entrée

CHICKEN SALAD WITH CURRIED MAYONNAISE
HERBED COTTAGE CHEESE
TOASTED ENGLISH MUFFINS

Dessert

JEAN'S BROWNIES
COFFEE

CHICKEN SALAD WITH CURRIED MAYONNAISE

4 cups bite-sized
  pieces cooked
  chicken breasts
1 cup coarsely chopped
  white stalks celery
Salt and fresh-ground
  pepper
¾ cup mayonnaise*
¼ cup sour cream
1 teaspoon grated
  onion (optional)

1–2 teaspoons curry
  powder
6 hard-cooked eggs
3 tomatoes peeled and
  quartered
Salad greens
French dressing 1*
¼ cup capers
Chopped parsley

Combine chicken and celery in a bowl. Season with salt and pepper. In a separate bowl blend together mayonnaise, sour cream, grated onion, and curry powder. Pour mixture over chicken and toss lightly. Cover and refrigerate. Halve eggs lengthwise, season with salt and pepper, and store with tomatoes in refrigerator on covered platter. Wash and dry salad greens, wrap in clean cloth, and put with rest of salad ingredients. Have capers drained and parsley at hand.

To assemble salad—toss greens in French dressing and arrange on shallow platter. Mound chicken in the center and surround with egg halves alternating with tomato wedges. Season again lightly with salt and pepper and sprinkle with parsley.

HERBED COTTAGE CHEESE

1 pound small-curd creamed cottage cheese
Salt and fresh-ground pepper
Chopped chives or scallion tops
Chopped dill or dried dill
Chopped parsley
Paprika

Blend cottage cheese with all ingredients except paprika. Correct seasoning and pile into a serving bowl. Sprinkle with paprika.

TOASTED ENGLISH MUFFINS

6 whole English muffins
Butter

Cut muffins in two by stabbing all the way around with a fork (this makes for an uneven surface that toasts well). Arrange on cookie sheet and toast under broiler just before serving lunch. Butter generously.

JEAN'S BROWNIES

¼ pound butter
3 squares bitter
chocolate
1 cup brown sugar
1 cup granulated
sugar

2 eggs lightly beaten
1 cup all-purpose
flour
½ cup chopped walnuts
or pecans
1 teaspoon vanilla

Melt butter and chocolate together. Cool. Mix together sugars, eggs, and flour. Blend well. Add butter-chocolate mixture and again blend well. Add nuts and vanilla. Bake in a 9-inch by 9-inch pan in a 350-degree oven for 28 minutes.

On the day before cook and bone the chicken breasts, make the mayonnaise, prepare the cottage cheese, and bake the brownies.

MENU 3

Entrée

EGGS BENEDICT

TOSSED GREEN SALAD

Dessert

GINGER PEAR COMPOTE

PECAN COOKIES

COFFEE

EGGS BENEDICT

1 tablespoon white
   vinegar
1 teaspoon salt
6 large eggs
6 slices boiled ham
   ¼ inch thick

3 hamburger rolls
   split in two
1¼ cups Hollandaise
   sauce*
Chopped parsley

Eggs Benedict are such a prime favorite that they are worth a little extra effort. You can poach the eggs early in the morning and store them in a bowl of warm water. Just before using, add boiling water so that they will be hot.

To poach—fill a medium-sized saucepan two thirds full of water. Add vinegar and salt and bring to a fast boil. Meanwhile, break 2 eggs gently into two cups. Remove fast-boiling water from heat and stir clockwise. When it is moving steadily, drop first one egg into the center, then the second, as fast as possible. Return pan to heat and bring to boil again. Then remove from heat and leave in pan until poached firm. With a slotted spoon, deposit eggs in pan of warm water and repeat until all eggs are poached.

To serve—heat ham in butter and toast the six hamburger roll halves. Place toasted rolls on ovenproof serving platter, cover each piece with a slice of ham and a poached egg, then spoon the Hollandaise sauce over. Glaze quickly under broiler. Sprinkle with parsley.

TOSSED GREEN SALAD

2–3 *varieties salad greens*	*French dressing 4**
Celery tops	*1 avocado*
¼ *pound baby spinach*	*2 tablespoons fresh lemon juice*
8 radishes	*1 ripe tomato*
¼ *pound mushrooms*	*Chopped parsley*

Wash and dry salad greens, celery tops, and spinach leaves. Slice radishes thin, halve mushrooms and trim stems, and marinate both together in a little of the French dressing. Peel avocado, slice thin, and sprinkle with lemon juice. Concass* the tomato and add to radishes and mushrooms. Store all ingredients in the refrigerator.

To serve—toss salad greens, celery tops, and spinach in French dressing. Add radishes, mushrooms, and tomatoes and toss gently again. Arrange salad on individual salad plates and arrange avocado slices over salad. Sprinkle with parsley.

GINGER PEAR COMPOTE

Juice from 12 canned
   pear halves
3 tablespoons fresh
   lemon juice
½ cup fresh orange
   juice
1 tablespoon each
   grated orange and
   lemon rind

2 teaspoons minced
   preserved ginger
¼ cup apricot brandy
   or orange curaçao
12 canned pear halves

Combine pear juice, lemon juice, orange juice, rinds of orange and lemon, ginger, and brandy or curaçao in a saucepan and bring to a boil. Add the pears and simmer for 15 minutes. Let cool to room temperature before placing in refrigerator to chill for several hours.

PECAN COOKIES

½ cup brown sugar
½ cup granulated sugar
1 cup Rice Krispies
1 cup chopped pecans

Pinch salt
1 egg white from
   large egg

Preheat oven to 350 degrees. Mix together brown and white sugar, Rice Krispies, pecans, and salt. Beat egg white until stiff

and shiny and fold into mixture. Drop by teaspoonfuls on a
buttered cookie sheet. Bake until lightly browned, about 13
minutes. Let stand 2 minutes, then remove from pan.

On the day before make the Hollandaise sauce, prepare the
salad ingredients (except the avocado), and make the compote
and cookies.

MENU 4

Entrée

FASHION PARK SALAD
SAVORY COTTAGE CHEESE
TOASTED ENGLISH MUFFINS*

Dessert

GLAZED FRUIT BOWL
DATE KISSES
COFFEE

FASHION PARK SALAD

6–8 slices of ham
   about ⅛ inch thick
6–8 slices Swiss cheese
2 heads iceberg lettuce
1 cup mayonnaise*

1 cup chili sauce
Salt and fresh-ground
   pepper
Chopped parsley

With a sharp knife, slice ham and Swiss cheese into long narrow strips (if too long, cut in two). Shred lettuce, cutting both ways. Blend mayonnaise and chili sauce and put into a covered bowl. Store all ingredients in refrigerator.

To assemble—put lettuce in bowl, add ham and cheese, and pour dressing over them. Toss until thoroughly blended. Season with salt and pepper and sprinkle with parsley.

SAVORY COTTAGE CHEESE

Stuffed olives   Salt and fresh-ground
Radishes   pepper
Raw carrot   Salad herbs
White celery stalks   Chopped parsley
1 pound small-curd
    cottage cheese

Finely chop olives, radishes, carrot, and celery. Add to the
cottage cheese. Season to taste with salt and pepper and add
whatever chopped fresh or dried herbs are available (such as
chives, dill, tarragon, etc.). Spoon into serving bowl and sprinkle
with chopped parsley.

GLAZED FRUIT BOWL

1 No. 2¼ can Elberta   ½ cup dark brown
    freestone sliced   sugar
    peaches   3–4 tablespoons orange
1 can purple plums   curaçao or sherry
    (1 pound, 14 ounces)   Cinnamon
1 No. 2½ can apricot   Grated rind of 1 orange
    halves   ½ pint sour cream
1 small can pitted
    dark cherries

Drain each can of fruit separately. Arrange in ovenproof dish in
two or three layers, sprinkling each layer with brown sugar,
curaçao, and a dash of cinnamon. Scatter orange rind across

the top. Bake in 350-degree oven for 30 minutes, basting occasionally. Turn off heat but let fruit remain in oven for another 30 minutes, again basting occasionally. Serve warm or at room temperature with a bowl of sour cream lightly sprinkled with cinnamon.

DATE KISSES

2 egg whites
⅛ teaspoon cream of
   tartar
Pinch salt
½ cup superfine sugar

½ teaspoon vanilla
¼ pound dates cut
   fine
½ cup chopped pecans

Beat egg whites until frothy, add cream of tartar and salt and beat until stiff and dry. Beat in sugar gradually for the first 6 tablespoons, then fold in the balance. Add vanilla, then fold in dates and nuts. Arrange by teaspoonfuls on a buttered, lightly floured cookie sheet. Bake in 350-degree oven for 25 minutes.

On the day before make the mayonnaise, prepare the savory cottage cheese (keep covered in the refrigerator) and bake the date kisses.

MENU 5

Entrée

HAMBURGERS ON TOAST

BROWNED ONIONS

TOMATO AND CUCUMBER SALAD

Dessert

PECAN CHOCOLATE CAKE

COFFEE

HAMBURGERS ON TOAST

*1½ pounds top round
    ground
Salt and fresh-ground
    pepper
1–2 teaspoons
    Worcestershire sauce
Garlic powder (optional)*

*1 teaspoon cold water
1 teaspoon chopped
    chives
1 teaspoon chopped
    parsley
9 slices white bread,
    crusts trimmed*

Let hamburger stand at room temperature for at least a half hour. Season with salt, pepper, Worcestershire sauce, and garlic powder to taste. Add water, chives, and parsley and blend lightly. Toast bread on one side, remove pan from oven, turn bread and butter untoasted side. Heap with seasoned hamburger, making sure entire bread slice is covered. Let stand until ready to put under broiler before serving.

BROWNED ONIONS

2 tablespoons salad oil   Salt and fresh-ground
1 tablespoon butter   pepper
4 large onions sliced   Paprika
   thin

In a heavy skillet heat oil and butter. Add onions, season with salt and pepper, and sprinkle lightly with paprika. Let cook slowly until a deep brown. Put aside until ready to reheat when broiling hamburgers. When hamburgers are broiled, cut in two and arrange on a platter with bowl of hot browned onions in the center.

TOMATO AND CUCUMBER SALAD

2–3 varieties salad   Salt and fresh-ground
   greens   pepper
3 long thin cucumbers   French dressing 1*
3 large ripe tomatoes   Chopped parsley

Wash and dry salad greens. Slice cucumbers thin, peeled or unpeeled, and store in bowl of ice water in the refrigerator for at least 1 hour. Peel tomatoes and cut into thick slices. Season with salt and pepper and marinate in a little French dressing. After 1 hour, drain cucumbers and press tightly between palms to eliminate water. Put in a bowl with French dressing, season with salt and pepper.

To assemble salad—toss greens in French dressing and arrange on individual salad plates. Put two tomato slices on each plate and spoon over with cucumbers. Sprinkle with parsley.

PECAN CHOCOLATE CAKE

3 squares bitter
   chocolate
¼ pound butter
3 eggs
1 cup sugar

½ cup pastry flour
Dash salt
1 teaspoon vanilla
1 cup chopped pecans

CHOCOLATE ICING

1 tablespoon butter
1 cup confectioners'
   sugar
1 square bitter
   chocolate, melted

½ teaspoon vanilla
2–3 tablespoons strong
   boiling coffee

Melt chocolate and butter in top of double boiler. Cool. Beat eggs and sugar until thick and lemon-colored. Sift together flour and salt. Add chocolate-butter mixture to egg mixture, blend well, then cut in sifted flour with a metal spoon. Add vanilla and nuts and pour into a buttered and floured 7-inch by 11-inch pan. Bake in a 375-degree oven 25–30 minutes (check with cake tester).

To make icing—cream butter. Add a little of the sugar, then the melted chocolate and vanilla. Blend well and add remainder of the sugar with enough coffee to make the icing the right consistency for spreading.

On the day before prepare the salad ingredients and bake the cake, but ice it on the day.

MENU 6

Entrée

TOMATO ASPIC SURPRISE
RYE BREAD TOAST

Dessert

COFFEE CAKE
COFFEE

TOMATO ASPIC SURPRISE

1 large can tomatoes
6 cloves
2 onions sliced
2 bay leaves
1 teaspoon salt
6 peppercorns
3 stalks celery coarsely
    chopped
2 tablespoons gelatin
½ cup cold water
2 tablespoons vinegar
1 tablespoon fresh lemon
    juice

1 teaspoon sugar
½ pound small-curd
    cottage cheese
Salt and fresh-ground
    pepper
1 tablespoon chopped
    chives
6 stuffed eggs
Salad greens
French dressing 4*
Chopped parsley

STUFFED EGGS

¼ cup mayonnaise*   6 hard-cooked eggs, shelled
1 tablespoon fresh lemon   Salt and fresh-ground
  juice   pepper
½–1 teaspoon curry
  powder

Boil together tomatoes, cloves, onions, bay leaves, salt, peppercorns, and celery until they are soft (about 30 minutes). Press
through sieve or food mill (there should be about 2 cups).
Soften gelatin in cold water, then dissolve in the hot mixture.
Add vinegar, lemon juice, and sugar. Pour into oiled ring
mold and chill. Season cottage cheese with salt and pepper.
Add chives, and when aspic is partially set, drop 8 heaping
tablespoons of cottage cheese at equal distances apart in aspic
ring. Let it continue to chill in refrigerator for several hours
until set.

To stuff eggs—mix together mayonnaise, lemon juice, and curry
powder. Halve eggs lengthwise, tip yolks into mayonnaise
mixture, and mash with a fork. Season to taste with salt and
pepper and fill whites with mixture. Press down with back of
fork to make a pattern, or pipe yolks into whites with small
pastry bag and ½-inch tube. Refrigerate, covered, until ready to
serve.

To assemble salad—wash and dry salad greens and toss in
French dressing. On a large platter arrange bed of lettuce
and unmold tomato ring in center. Surround with stuffed eggs
and sprinkle parsley over entire salad.

RYE BREAD TOAST

6–7 slices rye bread
Butter at room temperature

Trim crusts from rye bread and put on cookie sheet. Have broiler on so that when salad is assembled, toast can be quickly made, buttered, and sliced in two. Have bread basket ready at hand.

COFFEE CAKE

10 tablespoons butter
1 cup sugar
1 egg
1¾ cups pastry flour

2½ teaspoons baking powder
¼ teaspoon salt
1 cup milk
1 teaspoon vanilla

TOPPING

2 egg whites
1 cup dark brown sugar
½ cup chopped walnuts or pecans

Cream butter and sugar. Add the egg and beat until light. Sift together flour, baking powder, and salt and add to mixture alternately with milk. Continue beating for a few minutes. Add vanilla and pour in a shallow 9-inch by 9-inch buttered pan. Spread with topping and bake in 350-degree oven for 25–30 minutes.

To make topping—beat egg whites until stiff. Add sugar gradually and continue beating for a few minutes. Spread over cake batter and sprinkle with chopped nuts.

On the day before make the tomato aspic surprise and the coffee cake.

MENU 7

Entrée

CHEESE SOUFFLÉ
ASPARAGUS SALAD VINAIGRETTE

Dessert

PEACH KUCHEN
COFFEE

CHEESE SOUFFLE

6 slices fresh white bread   2½ cups milk
Butter   1 teaspoon dry mustard
1½ cups grated sharp   ½ teaspoon salt
   Cheddar cheese   ½–1 teaspoon
5 eggs well beaten   Worcestershire sauce

Trim crusts from the bread, butter the slices, and cut in two.
Butter an 8-inch soufflé dish and alternate layers of bread with
grated cheese. In a bowl mix together eggs, milk, mustard, salt,
and Worcestershire sauce. Whisk until well blended. Pour egg
mixture over bread and cheese layers and let stand, covered, for
at least 2 hours. Place dish in a pan of hot water and bake,
covered, in 350-degree oven for 1 hour.

ASPARAGUS SALAD VINAIGRETTE

2 cans green asparagus   Vinaigrette sauce*
   tips   1 hard-cooked egg
Salad greens   Chopped parsley
Salad herbs

Drain asparagus, put in flat shallow bowl, and pour over a marinade of vinaigrette sauce well blended and shaken. Refrigerate. Wash and dry salad greens, snip whatever herbs are available (chives, tarragon, chervil, dill, etc.), and store herbs in wax paper on top of salad greens. Refrigerate, covered. Grate hard-cooked egg and store with greens and herbs.

To assemble salad—toss greens in vinaigrette sauce and arrange on individual salad plates. Put three or four asparagus tips on each plate, spoon over a little additional sauce, and sprinkle with grated egg and parsley.

PEACH KUCHEN

2 cups Bisquick mix   3 10-ounce packages frozen
⅔ cup light cream   sliced peaches
2 tablespoons butter melted   ½ cup sugar
1 tablespoon sugar   Cinnamon
12 fresh peaches peeled   ¼ pound butter, melted
   and sliced
      OR

In a large bowl combine Bisquick mix, cream, melted butter, and sugar. Grease a regulation-sized cookie sheet and divide batter into six or eight parts on sheet. Lightly flour palms of hands and pat batter until entire sheet is covered with thin pastry. Arrange fresh or thawed peaches over pastry and sprinkle with sugar and cinnamon. Dribble melted butter over peaches. Bake in 400-degree oven for 15 minutes, or until lightly browned. Cut into large squares while still hot, but let remain in pan until cool.

On the day before prepare salad ingredients. Neither the soufflé nor the kuchen takes long to assemble. This soufflé is foolproof, and if it bakes an extra 10 or 15 minutes it makes no difference—hence there is no pressure at lunch time.

MENU 8

Entrée

SALAD NIÇOISE
TOASTED ENGLISH MUFFINS*

Dessert

SPONGECAKE

COFFEE

SALAD NICOISE

5 *ripe tomatoes peeled and quartered*

1 *red onion thinly sliced*

1 *cup canned whole green beans*

4 *hard-cooked eggs quartered*

1 *13-ounce can white tuna*

12 *anchovy fillets*

12 *pitted ripe olives*

Salad greens including Bibb lettuce if possible

*French dressing 4**

Salt and fresh-ground pepper

Chopped parsley

Prepare vegetables and eggs. Drain tuna and put, in chunks, in a bowl. Drain anchovies and olives. Wash and dry salad greens and store in refrigerator with vegetables, eggs, and tuna.

To assemble—toss greens very lightly in salad bowl in French dressing (more will be used later). Arrange tomatoes, onion, celery, beans, eggs, and tuna attractively on greens. Season with salt and pepper. Make a lattice of anchovies and set ripe olives between. Shake French dressing hard and sprinkle lightly over top of salad. Garnish with parsley.

SPONGECAKE

6 egg whites
1 teaspoon cream of tartar
½ cup sugar
6 egg yolks
1 teaspoon almond
  flavoring
1 tablespoon fresh lemon
  juice

¼ cup fresh orange juice
1¼ cups cake flour
1 cup sugar
½ teaspoon baking powder
¼ teaspoon salt
Confectioners' sugar

Beat egg whites with cream of tartar until foamy. Gradually add sugar and beat until very stiff. Mix together egg yolks, almond flavoring, lemon and orange juice, and beat until thick and lemon colored. Sift together flour, sugar, baking powder, and salt. With a metal spoon lightly fold flour-sugar mixture into egg yolk mixture. Fold in stiffly beaten egg whites. Pour into an unbuttered angel cake 9-inch tube pan and bake in a 350-degree oven 40–45 minutes. (Test by denting lightly with finger. If done, the cake will spring back.) Invert pan and let stand until cold. Loosen cake by running knife around the edges and turn out on a serving platter. Garnish with sifted confectioners' sugar.

On the day before prepare salad ingredients as much as possible and bake the spongecake. Do not sift the sugar over the cake until just before serving.

MENU 9

Entrée

HAM-CHEESE EGG PIE
TOAST POINTS*
SLICED CUCUMBERS

Dessert

MERINGUE CAKE
COFFEE

HAM-CHEESE EGG PIE

6 large eggs well beaten   ¾ cup diced cooked ham
⅓ cup light cream   ¾ cup grated sharp
6 tablespoons butter,   Cheddar cheese
   melted   18 green asparagus spears
3 tablespoons flour   fresh or canned
Salt and fresh-ground
   pepper

If using fresh asparagus, cook as in asparagus salad with caper dressing* and cut stalks so that they are about 5 inches long. Canned asparagus is very good with this dish.

Combine eggs, cream, 4 tablespoons butter (reserve balance), flour, salt, and pepper in a bowl and beat together until well blended. Stir in ham and cheese and pour mixture into a buttered 9-inch pie plate. Arrange asparagus spears like spokes over the top. Dribble remaining butter over asparagus and bake in 325-degree oven for 25 minutes, or until set. Let stand 10 minutes before cutting and then slice like a pie.

SLICED CUCUMBERS

4 long thin cucumbers
Salt
⅔ cup white vinegar
⅓ cup olive oil
½ teaspoon sugar
1 teaspoon water
Salt and fresh-ground
   pepper

2 tablespoons chopped
   chives
2 tablespoons finely
   chopped onion
Chopped parsley

Peel cucumbers, slice very thin, and put in a bowl which they fill to the brim. Salt well, cover with wax paper, and put some heavy object on the paper to press down the cucumbers. Refrigerate for at least 4 hours. In a jar mix together vinegar, oil, sugar, water, salt, and pepper. Shake well. Press the cucumbers by holding a handful at a time between both palms and squeezing out the water. When all are limp and pressed, place in a serving bowl and add the chives and onion. Pour over well-shaken salad dressing and correct seasoning. Sprinkle with parsley and refrigerate until ready to serve.

MERINGUE CAKE

2 packages ladyfingers
6 egg whites
⅛ teaspoon salt
2 cups sugar
1 teaspoon vanilla

1 quart starwberries or
    raspberries
½ pint heavy cream,
    whipped
1–2 tablespoons superfine
    sugar

Line the sides and bottom of a small springform pan with lady-fingers, putting the crust side next to the pan. Beat together egg whites and salt until stiff and dry. Beat in 1 cup of sugar and fold in balance of sugar and vanilla. Fill the lined spring-form with this mixture and bake in a 275-degree oven for 1 hour. Mash fruit, sweeten to taste with sugar, and cover top of meringue cake. Spread whipped cream (also sweetened to taste) over fruit.

On the day before prepare cucumbers but refrigerate overnight instead of for 4 hours. Make the dressing but do not combine them until *the* day. Bake the meringue cake and store in an airtight cookie tin. Add the fruit and whipped cream on *the* day.

MENU 10

Entrée

ITALIAN VEGETABLE SALAD

CREAM CHEESE MOLD

TOASTED CRACKERS

Dessert

PINEAPPLE SHERBET

BUTTERSCOTCH PECAN SQUARES

COFFEE

ITALIAN VEGETABLE SALAD

4 tomatoes peeled and
  quartered
2 cucumbers unpeeled
  and sliced thin
¼ pound fresh mushrooms
  sliced
French dressing 4*

Chopped parsley
4 hard-cooked eggs
  quartered
1 green pepper, core and
  seeds removed
½ red onion thinly sliced
Salad greens

In a shallow bowl marinate tomatoes, cucumbers, and mushrooms in a little of the French dressing. Sprinkle with parsley and refrigerate. Put hard-cooked eggs, thinly sliced pepper, and onion in another bowl. Cover. Wash and dry salad greens and refrigerate next to all other salad ingredients.

To assemble—toss greens in French dressing and arrange on a large platter. Put pepper and onion slices in same bowl and toss in any remaining dressing (or add a little more). Arrange tomatoes, cucumbers, mushrooms, eggs, pepper, and onion attractively on bed of lettuce. Season with salt and pepper and sprinkle with chopped parsley.

CREAM CHEESE MOLD

8-ounce package cream cheese at room temperature
2 tablespoons butter at room temperature
1 teaspoon capers
½ teaspoon lemon juice
1 teaspoon salt
1 teaspoon finely chopped chives
2 anchovies finely chopped
1 slice onion minced
Paprika

Blend together cheese and butter until smooth. Add remaining ingredients, except paprika, and mix lightly. Press into a small mold and let stand a few hours in refrigerator.

To serve—turn out onto plate, surround with crisp crackers, and sprinkle with paprika.

PINEAPPLE SHERBET

6 large scoops pineapple sherbet
Creme de menthe

For each serving, pour 1 tablespoon creme de menthe over scoop of pineapple sherbet.

BUTTERSCOTCH PECAN SQUARES

2 eggs
2 cups dark brown sugar
¼ pound butter melted and
   cooled
2 teaspoons vanilla

1⅓ cups all-purpose flour
2 teaspoons baking powder
Dash salt
1 cup coarsely chopped
   pecans

Beat eggs with a rotary or electric beater until they are frothy. Beat in sugar gradually and continue beating until mixture is smooth. Add melted butter and vanilla. Sift together flour, baking powder, and salt. Stir into egg mixture. Add pecans and pour the batter into a lightly oiled 9-inch by 9-inch baking pan. Bake in a 325-degree oven for 30–40 minutes, or until batter begins to pull away from sides of pan. Cool. Cut into squares. (If making the day before—store in an airtight cookie tin.)

On the day before prepare as much of the salad as possible, make the cheese mold (remove from refrigerator 2 hours before serving), and bake the butterscotch pecan squares.

5.

SALAD DRESSINGS AND SAUCES

+++

Salads offer a splendid opportunity for improvisation. The greater the variety, the greater the interest. Bibb, iceberg, Boston, oak leaf, and salad bowl are types of lettuce that, flanked by young spinach leaves, watercress, endive, chicory, or numerous other adjuncts add flavor and eye appeal. Salad dressings can be assembled in endless variety too. While the basic French dressing of three parts olive oil to one part vinegar (or fresh lemon juice) seasoned with salt, pepper, and a pinch of mustard is excellent, there are many tasty variations of this formula, such as the use of different kinds of vinegar—wine, herb, garlic, cider, tarragon, and many more. The addition of fresh herbs— dill, chervil, basil, tarragon, chives, lovage, parsley, etc., enliven a salad, and finely chopped red onion, chopped shallots, or minced onion are welcome additions (unless you happen to be anti-onion). Diced celery, chopped green pepper, and sliced radishes have crunch appeal. Grated hard-cooked eggs, riced cottage cheese, sliced or concassed tomatoes supply both garnish and flavor.

When making a heartier salad such as lobster, chicken, vegetable, tuna, chef, fruit, or dozens of others, it is important to have a good dressing for the greens and a contrasting one for

the main ingredient. Curried mayonnaise works wonders for
lobster and chicken, grated onion enhances the flavor of tuna,
fresh lemon juice in the French dressing improves vegetable
and fruit salads. Before arranging any of these salads, the greens
beneath should be tossed in the dressing of your choice. A bed
of undressed greens can spoil any salad.

Greens must be washed carefully and thoroughly dried. There
is a terry cloth salad bag on the market that is excellent for
keeping washed and dried lettuce fresh and crisp. The following are suggested dressings to which, of course, you can add
whatever pleases you. With few exceptions I make salad
dressings in small quantity and keep in a cool place (not the
refrigerator) in a jar with screw-on cover. *Shake hard before
using.*

FRENCH DRESSING 1

1 tablespoon lemon juice   Salt and fresh-ground
2 tablespoons wine vinegar   pepper
¼ teaspoon dry mustard   6–8 tablespoons olive oil

Mix together lemon juice, wine vinegar, mustard, and season
to taste with salt and pepper. Add olive oil slowly, beating with
a fork or small whisk until well blended. Store in jar.

FRENCH DRESSING 2

¼ cup lemon juice   ⅛ teaspoon garlic powder
½ cup olive oil   ½ teaspoon sugar
Salt and fresh-ground   ½ teaspoon dill weed
  pepper   ½ teaspoon water

Blend all ingredients in a jar and shake well. Correct seasoning before using.

FRENCH DRESSING 3

¼ cup wine vinegar
¾ cup olive oil
Salt and fresh-ground
  pepper

½ teaspoon dry mustard
½ teaspoon paprika
1 tablespoon chopped white
  onion

Place all ingredients in container of blender. Cover and run for 30 seconds. This is a good dressing to which to add Roquefort or blue cheese. Just crumble about 2 ounces in with other ingredients and blend as above.

FRENCH DRESSING 4

¼ cup wine vinegar
¼ cup garlic vinegar
1 cup olive oil
Salt and fresh-ground
  pepper

¼ teaspoon basil
¼ teaspoon tarragon
½ teaspoon Worcestershire
  sauce

Beat all ingredients together in a bowl or shake very hard in a jar.

TART FRENCH DRESSING

½ cup olive oil
¼ cup vinegar (cider,
   tarragon, and herb
   mixed)
1 teaspoon salt
½ teaspoon fresh-ground
   pepper
½ teaspoon sugar

½ teaspoon dry mustard
1 teaspoon Worcestershire
   sauce
2 teaspoons fresh lemon
   juice
1 teaspoon water
2 garlic buds peeled and
   slit

Beat all ingredients together except garlic buds. Bottle, add garlic buds to jar, and shake very hard before using.

VINAIGRETTE SAUCE

1 teaspoon salt
⅛ teaspoon fresh-ground
   pepper
Few grains cayenne
   pepper
¼ teaspoon paprika
¼ cup cider vinegar
¾ cup olive oil
1 tablespoon finely chopped
   pimiento

1 tablespoon finely chopped
   cucumber pickles
1 tablespoon finely chopped
   green pepper
1 tablespoon chopped
   chives
1 hard-cooked egg finely
   chopped (optional)

In a bowl or small mixer bowl combine salt, pepper, cayenne, and paprika. Slowly and alternately add the vinegar and olive oil. Add remaining ingredients, blend well, and put in a jar.

Good cold with green salad, fresh or canned asparagus. Good hot over fish, broccoli, fresh asparagus, Brussels sprouts, etc.

MAYONNAISE

Blender mayonnaise is so delicious and so quickly and easily made that any other method seems obsolete. When keeping house without a blender (which happens to me from time to time) I use a good brand of commercial mayonnaise to which I add fresh lemon juice and herbs. Warning! When not in use, mayonnaise should be kept in the refrigerator at all times, as it is subject to dangerous bacterial activity.

BLENDER MAYONNAISE

2 whole eggs
4 tablespoons fresh lemon juice or vinegar
1 teaspoon dry mustard
1 teaspoon salt
1 teaspoon garlic powder (optional)
⅛ teaspoon cayenne pepper
2 cups salad oil

Place eggs, lemon juice or vinegar, mustard, salt, garlic powder, and cayenne pepper into blender. Add ½ cup of oil. Put on cover and run blender for 5 seconds. Remove cover, turn on blender again (low speed if you have more than one) and slowly but steadily pour in balance of oil (1½ cups), stopping occasionally to stir with rubber spatula. When all the oil has been added (about 2 minutes after starting blender) run blender for 2 to 3 seconds more. Pour into a jar and refrigerate at once. Makes about 1½ cups.

HOLLANDAISE SAUCE (By hand)

Unlike mayonnaise, it is easy to make Hollandaise by hand, although much faster by blender.

3 egg yolks
2 tablespoons fresh lemon
    juice
1 teaspoon tarragon vinegar
1 teaspoon salt

Pinch dry mustard
¼ pound butter at room
    temperature, cut into
    thirds

Combine egg yolks, lemon juice, vinegar, salt, and mustard in top of double boiler and beat with an egg beater to blend. Place over hot (not boiling) water shallow enough not to touch the pan. Immediately add one third of the butter and beat until butter has melted and blended with other ingredients. Repeat with the other two thirds, never stopping beating. Continue beating until a good thickness has been reached, about 6 minutes altogether. If not using at once, stand it in a shallow pan of hot water. If, when ready to serve, it has thickened too much, thin with a little light cream or boiling water. Makes about 1 cup. Good over hot vegetables (asparagus, broccoli, etc.). Transforms poached eggs into eggs Benedict, adds zest to chicken sandwiches.

BLENDER HOLLANDAISE

½ pound butter
4 egg yolks
2 tablespoons fresh lemon
    juice

¼ teaspoon salt
Pinch cayenne pepper

In a small pan heat butter to the point of bubbling but do not let it burn. Into the blender container put egg yolks, lemon juice, salt, and cayenne pepper. Cover container and turn motor on low speed for 2 seconds (just long enough to blend the ingredients). Remove cover and pour the hot butter in a steady stream. When all the butter has been added, turn off motor. Makes about 1¼ cups.

MAGIC HOLLANDAISE

In the refrigerator chill:

1 heavy skillet	1½ teaspoons lemon juice
¼ pound butter	¼ teaspoon salt
2 large egg yolks	Pinch cayenne pepper

Put all the ingredients in the cold skillet and place over low heat. Rotate the butter around the skillet with a spoon. Continue stirring gently until butter is melted and mixture reaches a nice, thick consistency (miraculously it always does). If not serving at once, place in a pan over hot, not boiling, water to keep warm. Makes 1 cup.

BLENDER SAUCE BEARNAISE

2 tablespoons white wine	2 teaspoons chopped
1 tablespoon tarragon	shallots or onions
vinegar	¼ teaspoon fresh-ground
2 teaspoons chopped fresh	pepper
tarragon or ½ teaspoon	¾ cup Hollandaise sauce
dried	in blender

Combine wine, vinegar, tarragon, shallots, and pepper in a small saucepan, bring to a boil, and boil rapidly until almost all of the liquid has disappeared. Pour remaining concentrated brew into the Hollandaise sauce in the blender. Cover and blend on high speed for 6 seconds. Makes about 1 cup. Excellent on steaks, chops, and hamburgers.

QUICK BROWN SAUCE

1½ tablespoons butter
1½ tablespoons flour
2 cups beef stock or
* consommé*

Salt and fresh-ground
* pepper*

Melt butter in a heavy skillet, remove from heat, and add flour. Blend well, return to heat, and cook over low heat, stirring occasionally, until it is a good brown color. Add beef stock slowly, bring sauce to a boil, and cook for 5 minutes, stirring constantly. Lower the heat and simmer gently for 30–40 minutes, stirring occasionally. Skim off the fat and strain sauce through a fine sieve. Season to taste with salt and pepper. This sauce is good with leftover meat dishes—veal, lamb, or beef, or to strengthen or stretch meat gravy.

GARLIC LEMON SAUCE

2 cups red wine
1 onion finely chopped
2 cloves of garlic minced
2 tablespoons olive oil
2 tablespoons lemon juice

1 tablespoon chopped
* parsley*
Salt and fresh-ground
* pepper*

Cook wine, onion, and garlic in a small pan, uncovered, until reduced about one half. Add oil, lemon juice, parsley, salt, and pepper. Blend well. Serve over steak or hamburgers.

HARD SAUCE

12 tablespoons butter   3 tablespoons sherry
1½ cups confectioners' sugar
1 teaspoon fresh lemon
   juice

Cream butter, add sugar gradually, then lemon juice and sherry. Blend well. Pile lightly into serving bowl and swirl top into a peak. Refrigerate until 2 hours before serving—then let stand at room temperature. Good with any hot pudding, apple charlotte, etc.

CHOCOLATE FUDGE SAUCE

3 squares bitter chocolate   3 tablespoons light corn
¾ cup milk   syrup
¼ teaspoon salt   1 tablespoon butter
1½ cups sugar   ½ teaspoon vanilla

In a saucepan melt chocolate in milk over low heat, stirring constantly. Add salt, sugar, and corn syrup. Continue stirring and cook for 5 minutes. Add butter and vanilla. Blend well. Serve warm or cold over ice cream, cottage pudding, etc.

BUTTERSCOTCH SAUCE

1 cup light brown sugar   Dash salt
½ cup light corn syrup   ½ teaspoon vanilla
3 tablespoons butter   ½ cup evaporated milk

Simmer sugar, corn syrup, butter, and salt until mixture forms a firm ball when dropped in cold water. Remove from heat, add vanilla and evaporated milk. Blend well. Pour into a small bowl or pitcher before serving, blend again with a whisk. Serve warm or cold over ice cream or spongecake.

6.

RECIPES   RECIPES   RECIPES

✦✦✦

We who love cooking are avid collectors. We ferret, swap, and trade; we experiment, test, and improvise. After all, if we are going to be cooking three meals a day, they might just as well be challenging and delectable as monotonous and indifferent. I find that children, exposed to interesting, unusual food that is very much taken for granted (none of that "take a bite for Grandma" routine) not only eat everything in sight but develop sophisticated tastes that stand them in good stead all the days of their lives. They seem to bring a healthy curiosity and a minimum of prejudice to the new and untried, both in food and in other areas.

The recipes that follow have been tested on family, friends, and inn guests. None are too time-consuming, some are "quickies," all have passed the popularity test.

SOUPS

Before setting down a few soup recipes (there are several in Chapter 2) here are a few suggestions as to the garnishing and treatment of soup.

GARNISHES

No matter how delicious a soup may be, it will look bleak (especially a colorless variety) without benefit of some garnish. Whatever you have on hand will do—chopped parsley, chopped chives, paprika, crisp browned croutons, a thin slice of lemon, sliced egg, whipped cream (to which a pinch of salt has been added), diced avocado, minced watercress, a dollop of sour cream, or whatever else you fancy.

To prepare croutons—remove crusts from slightly stale white bread, cut in ½-inch cubes, and sauté in hot butter until they are an even brown on all sides. (The pan can be rubbed with garlic, if you choose, or grated onion can be added to the butter.) Drain cubes on a paper towel.

TIPS

Both sherry and Madeira improve most soups, but do not boil after adding wine.

To remove fat or grease from soup:

(1.) The easiest and best way is to make the soup the day before. When cool, put in refrigerator and by the following morning the fat will have hardened on the top of the bowl. Run a knife around the edge and fat can almost be lifted off whole. Spoon off any fragments. In addition, soup is usually better the second day, as flavors have had time to blend.

(2.) Drop a few ice cubes into the soup and remove them when the fat has adhered to them. Repeat.

(3.) Roll up a paper towel and use one end to skim off fat. As the end becomes coated with grease, cut off the used part and repeat.

If soup is too salty (which sometimes happens when canned consommé is used) add a raw potato, sliced, and bring to a boil. Remove the potato.

Given plenty of time, plenty of bones (beef, veal, and chicken), and many vegetables a fine consommé can be produced. Any basic cookbook carries a good recipe, but I find that it is usually more practical and considerably less work to use bouillon cubes and water or a good canned beef broth or consommé.

On the other hand, there is something very rewarding about chicken stock (perhaps it is the delicious meat available afterwards for sandwiches, salad, creamed chicken dishes, etc.). In any case, I make it often, use it with pleasure in a great variety of dishes, and store any extra in the freezer.

CHICKEN STOCK

1 stewing chicken (about 4 pounds)
2 chicken feet
1 teaspoon salt
6 peppercorns
Water
1 Bermuda onion stuck with 2 cloves
1 stalk of celery including green tops
2 sprigs parsley
1 bay leaf
2 carrots coarsely chopped
1 clove garlic
2 leeks (optional)

Wash chicken and chicken feet and put in a large saucepan. Add salt and peppercorns, cover with water, and bring slowly to a boil. Simmer for 1 hour with water barely bubbling. Skim scum from the surface from time to time. After 1 hour add onion, celery, parsley, bay leaf, carrots, garlic, and leeks. Continue to simmer for about 2 hours longer (or until chicken is tender). Strain liquid through a fine sieve. Remove fat and correct seasoning.

CREAM OF FRESH ASPARAGUS SOUP

2 pounds fresh asparagus
Water
3 tablespoons butter
1 medium-sized onion finely sliced
1 small clove garlic chopped
½ teaspoon fresh lemon juice
Celery tops
6 cups chicken stock
Salt and fresh-ground pepper
3 tablespoons butter
3 tablespoons flour
½ cup light cream
Paprika
Chopped parsley

Wash asparagus and cut off tips about a half inch from the top. Cook tips in a small pan covered with salted water until tender, about 15 minutes. Reserve drained tips and the water in which they were cooked. Slice remaining asparagus into 1-inch pieces (throwing away the coarse white end of each stalk). In a large deep saucepan melt butter, add onion, and sauté over low heat for 5 minutes. Add asparagus pieces, garlic, and lemon juice and cook very slowly, covered, until soft, about 20 minutes. Add the water that asparagus tips were cooked in, celery tops, chicken stock, and simmer, covered, for 40 minutes. Season to taste with salt and pepper. Put through food mill or sieve. Melt butter in a saucepan, remove from heat, and blend in flour. Return to heat and cook for a minute or two. Slowly add cream, then strained asparagus liquid. Simmer for 5 minutes. Correct seasoning and stand over hot water until ready to serve. Garnish with asparagus tips in each soup bowl and sprinkle with paprika and parsley.

VICHYSSOISE

6 leeks	Dash nutmeg
4 tablespoons butter	2 cups milk
1 medium-sized onion	1 cup light cream
finely sliced	3 tablespoons chopped
4 small potatoes sliced	chives
4 cups chicken stock	
Salt and fresh-ground	
pepper	

Remove green tops from leeks and cut the white part, crosswise, into ½-inch lengths. Melt butter in skillet and sauté leeks and onion until soft but not brown. Add potatoes and chicken stock and bring to a boil. Season to taste with salt, pepper, and nutmeg, and simmer, covered, 30–35 minutes. Scald milk and add to mixture, then bring soup just to the boiling point. Pour through sieve or food mill (or blend in electric blender 2 cups at a time) until smooth. Cool, then chill in refrigerator. Just before serving correct seasoning and add cream and a generous sprinkling of chives. Whisk to blend well and serve.

MUSHROOM AND ONION SOUP

4 tablespoons butter
2 bunches scallions
        OR
1 medium sized onion
1 clove of garlic (optional)
4 tablespoons flour

6 cups chicken stock
1 pound mushrooms
    chopped
½ cup light cream
Chopped parsley

Melt butter in saucepan. Slice scallions (including green tops) or onion, mince garlic*, and add both to pan. Cook until soft but not brown, about 5 minutes. Remove from heat and add flour. Blend well. Return to heat, bring to a boil for a minute or two, and slowly add stock to mixture. When soup begins to boil, reduce heat and simmer for 5 minutes. Put through a food mill or strainer together with the raw mushrooms. Return to heat and add cream. Heat through, and if not serving at once, put in top of double boiler over simmering water.

To serve—pour into soup bowls and garnish with parsley.

FRESH TOMATO SOUP

2 tablespoons butter
4 scallions thinly sliced
    OR
1 small onion chopped
1 clove of garlic minced*
6 ripe tomatoes cut into
    large pieces
1 carrot coarsely chopped
1 stalk celery sliced
Green celery tops
3 cloves

2 teaspoons sugar
6 cups consommé
Salt and fresh-ground
    pepper
Celery salt
3 tablespoons butter
3 tablespoons flour
1 avocado sliced
1 tablespoon fresh lemon
    juice
Chopped parsley

Heat butter in a deep pan and sauté scallions or onion and
garlic over low heat until soft, about 5 minutes. Add tomatoes
and simmer for 5 minutes. Add carrot, celery, celery tops,
cloves, sugar, and consommé. Season to taste with salt, pepper,
and celery salt and simmer, covered, for 30 minutes. Strain into
a bowl. In the empty pan melt butter, remove from heat, and
add flour. Return to heat, boil for a minute or two, then add
strained soup. Bring to a boil, then simmer for a few minutes.
Correct seasoning. Dice avocado and sprinkle with lemon juice
both to retain color and for flavoring. Pour soup into bowls,
garnish with diced avocado, and sprinkle with parsley.

BLENDER SOUPS

Here is an opportunity to improvise, create, and experiment
with no danger of catastrophe. Blender soup *always* turns out

well. In addition, here is a chance to dispose of those dibs and dabs that accumulate in the best of well-organized re-frigerators—food that is too good to be thrown out and too small in quantity to be useful. Any kind of base will do—tomato juice, consommé, milk, vegetable water, chicken broth, or a can of soup. To any of these you can add such tasty contributions as outer leaves of lettuce, cress, bits of cooked vegetables, cold meat, chicken, mushroom stems, parsley, celery leaves, cream sauce, cooked potatoes, rice, leftover gravy, soup—the list is endless. If you decide to add cream, do so at the very end and turn off blender as soon as cream has blended to avoid curdling. Taste—season—heat. It is amazing how delicious blender soup can be and what a satisfaction to the creator.

MEAT

JOHN'S LAMB BOWERY

1 6-pound leg of lamb	Dry mustard
Garlic slivers	Basil
Salt and fresh-ground pepper	Marjoram
Ginger	Bacon strips
	Ginger ale

GRAVY

2–3 tablespoons fat	1 teaspoon cornstarch
Pan juices	½ pint sour cream
1 cup consommé	½ bottle capers, drained

Let lamb stand at room temperature about 4 hours before roasting. Make a dozen slits in the meat and insert slivers of garlic. Blend together salt, pepper, ginger, mustard, basil, and marjoram and rub lamb all over with this mixture. Lay strips of bacon across the top and roast in a 350-degree oven for the first hour. Reduce heat to 300 degrees for balance of cooking, about 2 hours. Baste occasionally with ginger ale.

To make gravy—strain juices and skim off fat. Leave 2–3 tablespoons fat in the pan and bring to a boil. Add pan juices and consommé and stir briskly to include all particles in pan. Mix cornstarch with 3 tablespoons cold water, add to mixture, and boil gently for about 4 minutes. Add sour cream and capers, blend well, heat, and serve.

PATSY'S VEAL

½ cup flour
Salt and fresh-ground
  pepper
12 thin slices of veal, not
  pounded
Bacon fat or equal parts oil
  and butter

½–1 pound mushrooms
Butter
1 can beef consommé or
  chicken stock
½ cup sherry
Chopped parsley

Season flour with salt and pepper and dredge veal slices. Heat fat and brown on both sides a few at a time. Put into ovenproof casserole. Slice mushrooms and sauté in butter. Add stock and sherry to mushrooms, blend well, and pour over veal. Bake, covered, about 1 hour in a 350-degree oven. Sprinkle with parsley.

CHOPPED STEAK AND MUSHROOMS

1 small onion sliced thin
4 tablespoons butter
1 pound mushrooms sliced
  thin
1½ pounds ground round
  steak
1 cup sour cream

Salt and fresh-ground
  pepper
¼ teaspoon ginger
¼ teaspoon garlic powder
  (optional)
Chopped parsley

Sauté onion in butter until soft but not brown. Add mushrooms and cook over medium heat about 10 minutes. Stir ground beef into the pan and cook over medium heat until it is hot and cooked enough for your taste. During this time, probably 3–4 minutes, heat the sour cream, add salt, pepper, ginger, and garlic powder, and when hot, pour over the meat. Sprinkle with parsley.

FILLET (RECREATED)

Leftover fillet slices
¼ pound mushrooms for
   each 6 slices fillet
Butter
1 can condensed tomato
   soup

Salt and fresh-ground
   pepper
Béarnaise sauce*
Chopped parsley

Cut the leftover fillet into slices of desired thickness, wrap in aluminum foil, and heat in a 200-degree oven. Chop the mushrooms and sauté them quickly in 2–3 tablespoons butter. Add ¼–½ cup tomato soup to mushrooms, depending on how many you are using. Season lightly with salt and pepper. Remove the meat from the oven, spread each slice with mushroom mixture, and re-form the fillet on an ovenproof baking dish or copper pan. Cover with béarnaise sauce and run under the broiler for 2–3 minutes. Sprinkle with parsley.

CALVES' LIVER IN SOUR CREAM

6 large pieces calves' liver
  or 12 small pieces
Milk
Salt and fresh-ground
  pepper
4 tablespoons butter

½ cup oil
3 onions chopped
1 cup sour cream
3 tablespoons chopped
  chives
Paprika

Soak liver in milk for 2–3 hours, dry thoroughly, and season with salt and pepper. Melt one half the butter and the oil in a skillet. Add onions and cook until soft and slightly colored. Sauté liver in skillet with the onions until cooked through, or lightly pink, if you prefer. Heat sour cream but do not let it boil. Add chives, blend well. Remove liver from heat and pour sour cream mixture over. Stir and shake gently until cream and pan gravy are blended. Put liver on hot platter and pour over it the sauce remaining in the pan. Sprinkle lightly with paprika.

POULTRY

HERBED CHICKEN WITH LEMON

1 lemon

6 large half chicken breasts

Salt and fresh-ground
  pepper

Seasoned salt

4 tablespoons butter

4 tablespoons olive oil

4 shallots or green onions
  or 1 medium-sized onion

1 clove garlic minced*

½ cup dry white wine

2 tablespoons chopped
  parsley

1 teaspoon dried orégano

1 cup chicken stock

4 tablespoons butter

Chopped parsley

With a vegetable parer, pare off skin of lemon and cut into narrow strips. Squeeze the juice from lemon and reserve. Season chicken with salt, pepper, and seasoned salt. Heat 4 tablespoons butter and oil in large skillet and, when bubbling, add chicken (as many pieces as possible without crowding). Brown well on both sides and put into large iron casserole. Repeat until all breasts are browned and in casserole. Add a little butter to pan, if necessary, lower heat, and sauté shallots and garlic. Stir until golden, then add wine and stir well to loosen all particles in the skillet. Cook over medium heat until liquid is reduced by about half. Pour over chicken, then add parsley, orégano, lemon juice, stock, and lemon strips to casserole. Cover and cook slowly over medium heat for about 30 minutes, or until tender. Melt 4 tablespoons butter, pour over chicken just before serving. Sprinkle with parsley.

CHICKEN DIVAN

2 10-ounce packages frozen broccoli spears
4 tablespoons butter
4 tablespoons flour
2 cups chicken stock
½ cup heavy cream whipped
3 tablespoons sherry
Salt and fresh-ground pepper

½–¾ cup grated Parmesan cheese
6 large half chicken breasts cooked and sliced
       OR
Equal amount cooked turkey
Paprika
Chopped parsley

Cook broccoli according to directions on package less 2 minutes. Gently "refresh"* and place on bottom of large buttered oven-proof baking dish.

To make the sauce—melt butter in saucepan, remove from heat and blend in flour. Return to heat, bring to a boil, cook for a minute or two, then slowly add the chicken stock, stirring constantly until thick and smooth, about 5–6 minutes. Remove from heat and add cream, sherry, salt, and pepper. Pour one half of the sauce over the broccoli and add the grated cheese to the remainder of the sauce. Arrange chicken slices on broccoli and pour over remaining sauce plus a little extra cheese on top. Bake, uncovered, in a 375-degree oven for 30 minutes. Sprinkle with paprika and parsley.

Note: This entire dish can be made in the morning and baked in the evening. Keep in refrigerator but put at room temperature an hour before baking.

CHICKEN LIVERS MARGUERITE

½ cup flour
Salt and fresh-ground
  pepper
2 tablespoons oil
1½ pounds chicken livers
2 tablespoons butter

1 large onion coarsely
  chopped
½ pound mushrooms sliced
2 tablespoons sherry
Toast points*
Chopped parsley

Mix together flour, salt, and pepper and dredge chicken livers lightly. Heat oil and sauté livers, without crowding pan, until they are a good brown. Add more oil if necessary. In another pan melt butter, add onion, and cook over medium heat until soft but not brown. Add mushrooms to onion and cook for 5 minutes, stirring frequently and adding more butter if needed. Add livers and sherry and simmer all ingredients for another 5 minutes. Correct seasoning, serve on toast points, and sprinkle with parsley.

BAKED CHICKEN LEGS AND WINGS

6 small chicken legs
6 chicken wings
Dijon mustard
Salt and fresh-ground
  pepper

Sour cream
Fine dry bread crumbs
Parsley sprigs

Brush legs and wings lightly with mustard and season with salt and pepper. Brush each piece with sour cream and sprinkle over with bread crumbs. Place on baking sheet in one layer, cover with foil, and bake in a 400-degree oven for 30 minutes. Remove the foil and increase the heat to 450 degrees. Bake at this temperature for another 20 minutes, or until they are golden brown and tender when tested with a fork. Serve on a warm platter garnished with sprigs of parsley.

DUCK WITH CHERRIES

2 5-pound ducks quartered
Salt and fresh-ground
  pepper
Seasoned salt
¼ pound butter
1 No. 2 can pitted Bing
  cherries

2 cups juice from cherries
¾–1 cup port wine
½ cup juice from cherries
2 teaspoons arrowroot *or*
  cornstarch

Season ducks with salt, pepper, and seasoned salt. Melt butter in a large, heavy skillet and brown duck pieces, turning them often and pricking the skin so that the fat underneath can run out. Let ducks get dark and the skin crisp. Drain cherries and put juice in a measuring glass. When ducks are browned, tip out half the fat and add 2 cups of the cherry juice and the port wine. Cover and simmer for 1 hour or until ducks are thoroughly cooked and tender. Remove ducks to ovenproof platter and cover with aluminum foil. Skim the fat from the juices in the skillet and strain pan gravy into a saucepan. Mix together ½ cup juice from the cherries and arrowroot. Bring gravy in pan to a boil, add arrowroot mixture, bring back to a boil, then simmer for 2–3 minutes, or until slightly thick. Add drained cherries long enough to heat. Run pan with ducks under the broiler for 4–5 minutes to insure their being hot and crisp. Pour sauce into warm gravy boat.

FISH

With a few exceptions, such as shrimp, crab, lobsters, scallops, fish is not only difficult to serve to company (since it must be cooked at the last minute as a rule) but somehow never seems like a festive meal. We happen to live where a fine variety of fresh fish is available and consider a meal of flounder, mackerel, swordfish, sole, halibut, or scrod wonderful family fare, although we seldom offer it to guests unless requested to do so. We would serve the following recipes to anyone— our courage is born of past successes.

FILLETS OF FLOUNDER, CHABLIS SAUCE
(For 4)

8 *small onion rings*	4 *peppercorns*
8 *flounder fillets*	½ *bay leaf*
2 *tablespoons lemon juice*	½ *teaspoon salt*
½ *cup Chablis*	

SAUCE

1 *tablespoon butter*	2 *egg yolks*
1 *tablespoon flour*	1 *tablespoon water*
1 *cup liquid from flounder pan*	*Chopped parsley*

Butter a shallow baking dish, spread onion rings on bottom, and cover with flounder fillets. Sprinkle with lemon juice,

Chablis, peppercorns, bay leaf, and salt. Cover with a buttered sheet of aluminum foil. Bake in 350-degree oven for 15 minutes. Remove fillets to a warm, shallow, ovenproof dish and put in turned-off oven. Strain sauce from fillet pan into a measuring glass and add enough water, if necessary, to make 1 cup.

To make sauce—melt butter in saucepan, remove from fire, and add flour. Blend well, return to fire, bring to a boil, and slowly stir in the cup of liquid. Bring to a boil, then cook over medium heat until sauce has thickened, stirring constantly. Beat egg yolks with water and add to thickened mixture, stirring vigorously. Cook 1 minute. Pour sauce over fillets and set in a pan of boiling water in a 400-degree oven for about 3 minutes. Sprinkle with parsley. Serve immediately.

BAY SCALLOPS (For 4)

1½ pounds bay scallops *Paprika*
1 cup herbed bread crumbs *4 tablespoons butter*
Salt and fresh-ground *Lemon wedges*
    pepper

SAUCE

3 tablespoons butter
3 tablespoons fresh lemon juice
1 tablespoon chopped parsley

Spray scallops quickly with cold water and dry on paper towels. On wax paper spread out herbed bread crumbs (they can be purchased as such, but if not, add herbs—dill, parsley, chives, etc., to bread crumbs) and add salt, pepper, and paprika. Roll scallops in this mixture. Heat half the butter in a heavy skillet and, when foaming, add half the scallops, or as many as possible without crowding the pan. Cook quickly over high heat, stirring, until a golden brown, about 3 minutes. Remove to shallow oven-proof platter and repeat until all are cooked. Run platter under broiler for about 3 minutes while making sauce.

To prepare sauce—in a small pan heat butter, lemon juice, and parsley. Pour over scallops just before serving. Serve with lemon wedges.

BOILED LOBSTERS WITH DRAWN BUTTER

Many years ago my mother-in-law attended a lecture given by the famous restaurateur, Henri, of New York and Lynbrook fame, and brought home the astonishing news that lobsters mind being plunged into boiling water just as much as humans, and show their resentment by becoming tense and tough. The correct method, she reported, is to lull them to sleep, and we have found it to be the very best. Heres how:

6 1¼–1½ pound lobsters   *½ pound butter clarified*
Coarse salt   *6 parsley sprigs*
6 large lemons

Put lobsters in a large pot with cold water to cover. Add 1 tablespoon coarse salt for each gallon of water, or use salt water if available. Cover the pot, turn the heat on high, and go about your business until the water boils, about 40 minutes. Meanwhile, the relaxed lobsters go drowsing off to emerge, eventually, as tender delicacies. When the water comes to a good rousing boil, let them boil for 10 minutes (slightly longer for larger lobsters). Remove them to a table (covered with newspaper) right side up and let them drain. Cover with a large beach towel to keep warm. Lobsters should be warm but never hot. Cut lemons in large wedges with a sharp knife, then cut off the white pith along the cut edge. This both improves their appearance and prevents the juice from squirting.

To clarify butter—put in top of double boiler over simmering water and allow butter to melt without stirring. When ready to serve, pour butter gently into warm individual sauce dishes to accompany the lobsters. The sediment will remain in the bottom of the pan.

To serve lobsters—with the lobsters still standing right side up, cut with a sharp knife from the mark in the middle of the back right through the hard shell and the tail. The tail will curve in bowlegged fashion. Remove the black or grayish line of entrail. Put lobsters on a platter, still right side up, and garnish inside tail with lemon wedges at one end and sprig of parsley at the other. Be sure that accompanying clarified butter is *hot!* Serve lobsters with paper or terry-cloth bibs, plenty of paper napkins, individual picks and nutcrackers, and a receptacle in the center of the table into which to toss shells. Big advantage to wear old clothes.

COLD SCALLOPS PIQUANT

1½ pounds bay scallops
1 small onion sliced
2 parsley sprigs
2 dill sprigs or dried dill
White wine
6 ripe tomatoes

Salad greens
French dressing 1*
Salt and fresh-ground
    pepper
Chopped parsley

SAUCE

1 cup mayonnaise*
½ cup sour cream
2 tablespoons finely
    chopped chives
2 tablespoons finely
    chopped parsley

¼ teaspoon garlic powder
1 tablespoon fresh lemon
    juice
Salt and fresh-ground
    pepper

To prepare scallops—spray quickly with cold water and put them in a saucepan with onion, parsley, dill, and enough wine to cover. Bring liquid to a boil and simmer for about 3–4 minutes, or until scallops are white. Drain, cool, and refrigerate until very cold. Peel tomatoes and slice each into two thick slices. Toss salad greens lightly in French dressing and arrange on individual plates. Put two slices of tomato on each plate, season with salt and pepper, and cover with scallops. Pour over sauce and sprinkle with parsley.

To prepare sauce—blend all the sauce ingredients together in a small bowl. Season to taste with salt and pepper and chill.

COLD LOBSTER PIQUANT

2 2-pound lobsters boiled	½ teaspoon garlic powder
Hard-cooked yolks of 4 eggs	¼ teaspoon Worcestershire sauce
2 tablespoons chopped parsley	4 tablespoons wine vinegar
1 teaspoon chopped chives	1 cup olive oil
1 teaspoon chopped tarragon	½–1 teaspoon sherry
Salt and fresh-ground pepper	Salad greens
¼ teaspoon dry mustard	French dressing 1*
	4 ripe tomatoes quartered
	Extra chopped parsley

Slice the meat of the tail and claws into large bite-sized pieces. In the small bowl of the electric mixer, or by hand with a whisk mix together egg yolks, parsley, chives, tarragon, salt, pepper, mustard, garlic powder, and Worcestershire sauce. Add a little oil and start blending slowly. Alternate adding vinegar and oil, and continue mixing until sauce is fairly thick. Add sherry and blend well. In a salad bowl toss the salad greens lightly in French dressing. Make bed of greens on individual plates and arrange lobster meat on top. Pour sauce over it. Put tomatoes in salad bowl in remaining dressing (or add a little more) and season with salt and pepper. Garnish salad with the tomato wedges, and sprinkle chopped parsley over each plate.

VEGETABLES

JOHN'S SPINACH

2 packages frozen chopped
   spinach
3–4 tablespoons heavy
   cream
4 beef cubes

2 chicken cubes
1 tablespoon butter
1 medium-sized onion finely
   chopped
3 hard-cooked eggs sliced

Put spinach in saucepan with cream and soup cubes. Stir a
little while defrosting and separate spinach with a fork. Melt
the butter in a small skillet and sauté onion until soft but not
browned. When spinach is completely thawed, add sautéed
onion and cook together for 2 minutes. If necessary (*be sure
to taste!*), season with salt and pepper (cubes are salty so
check carefully). Keep hot in top of double boiler and serve
in a warm, shallow vegetable dish, garnished with egg slices.

GREEN BEANS IN TOMATO SAUCE

¾ cup olive oil
1½ cups onions thinly
   sliced
2 cups fresh tomatoes
   quartered
     OR
2 cups canned tomatoes

Salt and fresh-ground
   pepper
¼ teaspoon dried orégano
1½–2 pounds green beans,
   washed, ends snapped
   off, and cut in two

In a saucepan heat oil and sauté onions until soft and transparent, about 5 minutes. Add tomatoes, salt, pepper, orégano, and beans. Bring to a boil, cover, and cook over low heat for 1 hour. Remove cover for last 10 minutes. Serve hot or cold.

DUTCH CABBAGE

1 small head cabbage	Salt and fresh-ground
3 stalks white celery	pepper
4 tablespoons butter	3 tablespoons chopped
2 tablespoons wine vinegar	parsley
1 tablespoon sugar	

Shred cabbage very fine and slice celery, crosswise, in ¼-inch pieces. Rub a thick heavy pan generously with butter, add cabbage, celery, vinegar, sugar, and season well with salt and pepper. Cover with buttered wax paper and then a lid. Cook slowly until tender, about 20–25 minutes. During cooking test by using two forks to fluff up and redistribute vegetables in the pan. During final fluff up, add parsley and correct seasoning.

ONION RINGS

6 Bermuda onions	Salt and fresh-ground
1–2 cups milk	pepper
½ cup flour	Seasoned salt
	Oil

Peel onions, slice thin, and separate into rings. Soak in milk to cover for about 15 minutes. Drain and dry on paper toweling. Mix together flour, salt, pepper, and seasoned salt on wax paper and roll onions in the mixture. Heat oil until smoking hot—then fry onions. When brown and crisp, drain on brown paper. Keep warm in low oven until all are cooked.

MUSHROOMS IN CREAM

3 tablespoons butter
1 medium-sized onion
   finely chopped
1 pound mushrooms sliced
Salt and fresh-ground
   pepper

1 teaspoon flour
½–¾ cup heavy cream
   warmed
Chopped parsley

Melt butter in a heavy skillet and sauté the onion until soft but not brown. Add mushrooms and cook over medium heat for 4–5 minutes. Season with salt and pepper and add flour. Blend well. Add cream and simmer mushrooms in the cream until sauce has thickened slightly, about 2–3 minutes. Pour into warm vegetable dish and sprinkle with parsley.

EGGPLANT ZUCCHINI MELANGE

1 medium-sized eggplant
Salt
6 tablespoons olive oil
3 medium-sized zucchini
   thinly sliced
¼ cup chopped onion
2 cloves of garlic minced*

4 tablespoons dry bread
   crumbs
2 tablespoons chopped
   parsley
½ pound mushrooms sliced
   thin

Peel the eggplant and cut into 1-inch cubes. Sprinkle with salt and let stand, weighted by a plate, for 30 minutes. Drain well and dry on paper towel. Heat 2 tablespoons olive oil in skillet and brown cubes on all sides. Remove and keep warm. Heat 2 more tablespoons of oil in skillet and sauté zucchini for 10 minutes, or until tender. Season with salt and pour into pan with eggplant. Heat remaining 2 tablespoons oil in skillet and sauté onions until soft, not brown (3–4 minutes), stirring over medium heat. Add garlic, bread crumbs, and parsley to onion and cook for 3 minutes over low heat, stirring constantly. Sauté mushrooms and add to pan. Correct seasoning. Arrange eggplant and zucchini in ovenproof serving dish and spoon the mixture in the skillet over them. Put into hot oven or under broiler for a few minutes to make sure that vegetables are hot.

BAKED TOMATOES STUFFED WITH CUCUMBERS

4 tablespoons butter

4 tablespoons water

2 cucumbers peeled and coarsely chopped

2 teaspoons grated onion

4 teaspoons fresh lemon juice

Salt and fresh-ground pepper

6 ripe tomatoes

Dill

Buttered bread crumbs*

Chopped parsley

In a saucepan heat butter and water and add cucumbers, onion, and lemon juice. Season with salt and pepper and simmer for 5 minutes. Meanwhile cut off tops of tomatoes, remove pulp and seeds, and turn upside down on a paper towel to drain. When cucumbers are cooked, turn tomatoes right side up and season with salt, pepper, and dill. Fill tomatoes

with the cooked cucumber and sprinkle tops with buttered
bread crumbs and chopped parsley. Bake in a 400-degree oven
until tomatoes are tender and the crusts are brown, about 8–10
minutes.

CAULIFLOWER WITH CAPERS AND LEMON BUTTER

2 *small heads cauliflower*	3 *tablespoons washed*
4 *tablespoons butter*	*capers*
⅓ *cup fresh lemon juice*	*Finely chopped chives*
	Chopped parsley

Separate the flowerets and wash cauliflower in slightly salted
lukewarm water. Drain, rinse in cold water, and cook over
medium heat in salted water to cover until tender, about 15–20
minutes. Meanwhile melt butter in small saucepan over low
heat and add lemon juice, capers, and chives. Spoon cooked
cauliflower into warm vegetable dish and pour the sauce over it.
Sprinkle with parsley.

CORN AND TOMATO CASSEROLE

3 *cups uncooked corn*	2 *tablespoons butter*
kernels	*Salt and fresh-ground*
6 *ripe tomatoes*	*pepper*
Basil	*Sugar*
3 *tablespoons finely sliced*	1 *cup fresh bread crumbs*
onion	3 *slices lean bacon diced*
1 *green pepper seeded and*	*Chopped parsley*
finely chopped	

Cut and scrape the kernels from enough ears of uncooked corn to measure 3 cups. Butter a casserole or baking dish and line the bottom with one half the corn. Cover with 3 of the tomatoes thickly sliced and sprinkle lightly with basil. Scatter one half of the onion and pepper over the tomatoes, dot with one half of the butter, and season with salt, pepper, and a pinch of sugar. Cover layer with remaining corn and repeat with tomato, onion, and pepper. Shake bread crumbs over top of casserole and arrange diced bacon on top. Bake in 375-degree oven for 45 minutes. Sprinkle with parsley.

DESSERTS

CHOCOLATE TORTE

5 *egg yolks*
1 *cup sugar*
½ *cup cake flour*   ⎫
½ *cup cocoa*   ⎬ *sifted together*
1 *teaspoon baking powder* ⎭
½ *cup water*
5 *egg whites*
1 *teaspoon vanilla*

FILLING AND FROSTING

1 *pint heavy cream*   *Brandy or vanilla, instant*
2 *tablespoons cocoa*   *coffee, or rum*
4 *tablespoons superfine*   *Shaved chocolate*
   sugar

Beat egg yolks until blended. Add sugar and continue beating until thick and lemon-colored, about 6 minutes in mixer. Add sifted flour, cocoa, baking powder mixture alternately with water. Beat egg whites very stiff and fold in gently. Add vanilla. Bake in two 8-inch cake pans, greased and lined with wax paper in a 350-degree oven for 30 minutes. Test with a cake tester.

To make filling and frosting—combine cream, cocoa, and sugar and let stand in refrigerator for at least 2 hours. Whip together until stiff, add brandy or preferred flavoring to taste, and spread part on one layer. Cover with other layer and spread more thickly over top. Garnish with shaved chocolate.

MAPLE MOUSSE

1 cup sugar	Pinch salt
1 cup unblanched almonds	1 pint heavy cream
1 cup pure Vermont maple	whipped
syrup	1 teaspoon vanilla
5 egg yolks beaten	

Caramelize sugar and almonds as in praline powder* and, when cold and hard, pulverize. Cook together maple syrup, egg yolks, and salt until thick. Cool. Add almond powder and whipped cream, flavored with vanilla. Pour into a mold and freeze.

DATE AND WALNUT TORTE

2 eggs	¼ teaspoon vanilla
1 cup sugar	1 cup chopped walnuts
2 tablespoons cream	1 cup finely cut dates
2 tablespoons flour	½ pint heavy cream
1 teaspoon baking powder	A few grated walnuts

Beat eggs until light, add sugar and cream, and continue beating until well blended. Sift together flour and baking powder and fold into mixture. Add vanilla, nuts, and dates. Bake in greased, floured, 8-inch cake tin in a 325-degree oven for 50 minutes. Test with a cake tester. Cool. Cover with whipped cream and garnish with grated walnuts.

Ever since I began this book, my husband has insisted that I include crêpes pralinée. My resistance stems from the fact that they take a lot of time, although they can be made ahead in easy stages. He claims (and I do agree) that there is no better dessert, that it is universally popular, and that this book will be incomplete without it. As a clincher he reminded me of a May night a few years ago. We were alone at the inn, not yet open for the season, no staff, when along came a Frenchman and his wife looking for a place to stay for the night. No other place was open either—how could we refuse to take them in? Feeling very much a peasant, I went out into the garden to pick dinner. Into my basket went tender young ruby and Bibb lettuce, dill, chives, parsley, and two or three pounds of beautiful fresh asparagus. Our hamburger turned into chopped steak and mushrooms*. Blender Hollandaise* glamorized the fresh-picked asparagus, new potatoes were in hand (tossed in chopped dill, salt, and pepper), but the crowning glory emerged from the freezer in the form of a package of crêpes pralinée. Lightly brushed with melted butter, they went, frozen, into a 425-degree oven and within 10 minutes were transformed into a culinary triumph. Sifted confectioners' sugar added the final touch, and occasional Christmas cards from our delighted guests still happily recall those crêpes. I learned how to make them at the London Cordon Bleu and—well, here goes.

CREPES PRALINEE (40 filled crepes)

BATTER (Basic for breakfast pancakes, crêpes Suzette, crêpes stuffed with lobster, chicken, etc.)

1½ cups all-purpose flour
Pinch salt
2 whole eggs
2 egg yolks

20 ounces milk
2½ tablespoons melted
  butter

Sift flour and salt together into a large bowl. With fingers make a large well in the center and deposit whole eggs and yolks in the middle. Start mixing with a whisk while gently working milk and flour into the eggs. While some of the flour and milk are still unworked, add the melted butter and then, slowly, the balance of the flour and milk. If still a little lumpy when all ingredients are mixed together, whisk a little longer. Refrigerate for at least 1 hour.

PRALINE POWDER

1 cup unblanched almonds
1 cup superfine sugar

PRALINE BUTTER

8 ounces sweet butter at
  room temperature
1 cup superfine sugar

10 tablespoons praline
  powder
Brandy

To make crêpes—heat a 7- or 8-inch Teflon or omelet pan and when hot, grease lightly with oil or Crisco. Pour a small amount of chilled batter into the hot pan, tip pan, and roll batter around until entire pan is thinly covered. When underside is a good brown, loosen one edge and turn quickly with fingers or narrow spatula. When second side is browned, turn pan over on to cake rack (so that bottom side is up) and cover crêpe with a clean dish towel. Repeat until batter is finished. After a little practice it is easy to keep two pans going at once, which saves time.

To make praline powder—put almonds and sugar into a heavy skillet. Set over low heat. Do *not* stir. When sugar begins to melt, stir gently with a metal spoon until it is a good nut-brown color and almonds are entirely coated. Turn out on to an oiled pan or cookie sheet. Leave until mixture cools and hardens—then break into pieces and pound (or grind in blender) until pulverized.

It is a good idea to double or triple this praline powder recipe, and then you are ready for the next batch of crêpes as well.

To make praline butter—cream butter and gradually beat in sugar. Continue beating until mixture is white and well-beaten. Add praline powder and brandy to taste.

To fill crêpes—spread a teaspoonful of praline butter over crêpe and roll up into narrow cigars. Place them, slanting, on a buttered, ovenproof dish (extra crêpes can be frozen, filled). Brush with melted butter and put into a 400–450-degree oven for about 5 minutes, or until sizzling hot. Sift powdered sugar over dish before serving.

CHOCOLATE ROLL

5 egg yolks	5 egg whites stiffly beaten
1 cup sugar	2 tablespoons confectioners'
¼ cup dark cocoa	sugar
¼ cup flour	2 teaspoons cocoa
1 teaspoon vanilla	1 cup heavy cream

CHOCOLATE ICING

2 ounces butter at room	2 tablespoons dark cocoa
temperature	2 tablespoons brandy
4 cups confectioners' sugar	1 teaspoon cream

Preheat oven to 350 degrees. Beat yolks 1 minute, add sugar, and beat until pale yellow and mousselike, about 5 minutes. Mix together dark cocoa and flour and add to mixture. Add vanilla and when well blended fold in stiffly beaten egg whites. Butter a shallow 10-inch by 15-inch cookie sheet and line bottom with wax paper. Lightly butter wax paper and spread batter in pan, pushing to corners. Bake for 15 minutes. Immediately run a narrow spatula or butter spreader around inside rim to loosen sides. Combine confectioners' sugar and cocoa and sift over top of cake. Cover with wax paper and then a clean dish towel and, holding towel taut, flip pan over. Peel off wax paper lining and immediately roll up the cake (like a jelly roll) in the wax paper covering, and roll towel over cake so that it keeps the roll firmly intact over the wax paper. Before serving, unroll and spread with sweetened whipped cream and roll up again. Cover top and sides with chocolate icing and arrange on serving platter.

To make icing—cream butter, slowly add confectioners' sugar, and beat until smooth and well blended. Add cocoa and brandy and beat 1 minute more. Add cream, which helps make icing easy to spread. If still too thick, add a little more cream.

CHEESE CAKE (For 12)

1 package cornflake crumbs
1½ pounds cream cheese
1 14-ounce can sweetened
  condensed milk
4 large egg yolks
1 cup sour cream
1 tablespoon confectioners'
  sugar

1 teaspoon vanilla or fresh
  lemon juice
1 teaspoon grated lemon
  or orange rind
4 egg whites
¼ teaspoon salt

Butter 10-inch springform pan and line bottom and sides with cornflake crumbs. In an electric mixer beat together cream cheese and condensed milk. Continue beating and add egg yolks (one at a time—beating well after each addition), and continue beating until mixture is smooth. At lowest speed add sour cream, confectioners' sugar, vanilla or lemon juice, and rind. Blend well. Beat egg whites with salt until very stiff, then gently fold into cheese mixture. Pour batter into springform and bake in 275-degree oven for 1 hour. Turn off heat but *do not open oven DOOR* for 1 hour more. Let cake cool completely in oven—do not remove until it is cold. Transfer to platter and if not serving within an hour or two, refrigerate until an hour before serving.

SQUARES AND BARS

MERINGUE BUTTERSCOTCH BARS

4 tablespoon butter
1 cup dark brown sugar
1 egg
½ teaspoon vanilla

¾ cup all-purpose flour
   sifted
½ teaspoon salt
¼ teaspoon nutmeg

TOPPING

1 egg white
1 tablespoon light corn
   syrup

½ cup sugar
½ cup chopped walnuts

Combine butter and brown sugar in a saucepan and stir over low heat until mixture bubbles. Cool. Add egg and vanilla and blend well. Sift together flour, salt, and nutmeg and fold into mixture. Spread in buttered 8-inch by 8-inch pan. Spread topping over dough and bake in 350-degree oven for about 30 minutes.

To make topping—beat egg white and gradually add corn syrup. Then slowly add sugar, beating to very stiff peaks. Fold in chopped nuts.

DATE BARS

1 cup chopped walnuts
1 package dates finely cut
1⅓ cups cake flour sifted
1 teaspoon baking powder
4 egg yolks

1¼ cups sugar
4 egg whites
1 teaspoon vanilla
Powdered sugar

Put walnuts and dates in a bowl. Sift together flour and baking powder and add to walnuts and dates. Beat egg yolks for 1 minute and add to bowl. Add sugar and blend well. Fold in stiffly beaten egg whites and add vanilla. Bake in a shallow square 8-inch by 8-inch pan (lightly greased and lined with wax paper) for 35–40 minutes. When slightly cool, cut into bars and roll in powdered sugar. (Will keep fresh for several days if kept in an airtight cookie tin with wax paper between layers.)

CINNAMON NUT SQUARES

½ pound butter
1 cup dark brown sugar
1 egg yolk
2 cups flour

1 teaspoon cinnamon
1 egg white
½ cup chopped pecans

Cream butter and sugar, beat in egg yolk, and fold in flour and cinnamon sifted together. Pat into thin dough in a square 8-inch by 8-inch pan. Beat egg white for 1 minute and spread over dough. Sprinkle with chopped pecans and bake in 250-degree oven for 45 minutes. Cut into squares while hot.

COCONUT SQUARES

½ pound sweet butter   2 cups flour
½ cup dark brown sugar   ⅛ teaspoon salt

TOPPING

2 eggs   ½ cup coconut
1 cup dark brown sugar
1 cup walnuts, finely
   chopped

Cream butter and sugar. Sift together flour and salt and fold into mixture. Pour into a shallow 8-inch by 8-inch baking pan and bake in a 325-degree oven for 15 minutes. Remove from oven and spread on topping. Sprinkle with coconut and return to 325-degree oven for another 15 minutes. While still warm cut into squares or bars.

To make topping—blend together eggs, sugar, and nuts until thoroughly mixed.

MISCELLANEOUS

MOLLY'S ICED TEA

This is the third book of mine in which this recipe appears, because I have never found another as good. It keeps, bottled, in the refrigerator about a week, but its life expectancy during the summer is never that long.

20 *cups of water*	1 *cup orange Pekoe tea*
10 *oranges*	1 *large bunch mint*
7 *lemons*	3 *scant cups sugar*

Bring water to a fast boil. Meanwhile wash oranges and lemons, squeeze them into a bowl together, reserve the juice, and deposit the rinds in a huge pan. Add tea and mint to the pan, and when the water is boiling hard, pour over rinds. Let stand 1 hour. Into the pan that held the boiling water put sugar and strained fruit juice. At the end of 1 hour squeeze rinds with hands and shake (to obtain all juice) and throw away. Remove mint and strain the tea into the pan with sugar and fruit juice. Stir well to dissolve sugar. When cool, bottle and refrigerate.

To serve—put ice in tall glasses but do not put tea in a pitcher with ice (to avoid dilution). Shake well before pouring into glasses.

STRAWBERRY PRESERVE

This simple recipe produces a perfect strawberry preserve.

1 *pound strawberries*
1 *pound sugar*

Wash berries and hull them. Put in a saucepan with sugar and bring to a boil. Boil exactly 12 minutes. Pour onto a silver platter and let stand overnight. Sterilize jars, fill, and seal.

GRAPEFRUIT PRESERVE

2 *grapefruit*
2 *cups sugar*
2 *lemons*

Cut grapefruit from the top down and then cut the sections into smaller slices from the top down. Put in a large bowl, cover with water, and soak overnight. The following morning drain the fruit and pour into a large pan. Add the sugar and bring to a boil over low heat, stirring occasionally until the sugar has dissolved. Increase heat to medium and cook for 45 minutes, stirring a few times. Meanwhile grate the rind of the lemons and squeeze and strain the juice. At the end of 45 minutes add both rind and juice to pan and cook for 10 minutes longer. Bottle in sterilized jar and seal. Very good with chicken or duck.

PEACH CANTALOUPE PRESERVE

4 *lemons*
1 *heaping quart peaches peeled and diced*

1 *heaping quart cantaloupe peeled and diced*
6 *cups sugar*
⅛ *teaspoon salt*

Cut up lemons into small chunks and put in saucepan, covered with cold water. Bring to a boil and boil for 10 minutes. Drain and purée in blender for 1 minute. Put fruit in large greased (to avoid sticking) pan. Add sugar, puréed lemon, and salt and cook slowly until it boils, stirring occasionally. Boil hard for 40–45 minutes, or until thick, stirring constantly. Pour into hot sterilized jars and seal.

7.

TIPS AND SHORTCUTS

+++

Entertaining is easy when most of the work can be done ahead at a leisurely tempo. It also helps if the stage is set, so to speak, and some of the small, time-consuming jobs are out of the way before you even begin to work.

For example—fresh lemon juice in a convenient jar in the refrigerator is a boon every day in the week, entertaining or no. It improves everything it touches (salad dressings, sauces, vegetables, etc.) but can bring you to a dead stop if you are busily cooking and come up against a recipe that calls for 2 tablespoons of the precious stuff when none is at hand. While on the subject of lemon juice I would say that, in cooking, ersatz lemon juice is to fresh what "cooking wine" is to vintage. Neither should ever be allowed in the kitchen.

Chopped nuts and onions are also nuisances to prepare in the middle of cooking. Keep the former in jars (both finely and coarsely chopped) and the latter in a frozen ball in the freezer top of the refrigerator. It is easy to scrape off any given amount right into the skillet where it will defrost at once.

We come now to parsley. As you may have gathered, I am a parsley buff. I like it on practically everything. (This was carried to the nth degree by my family last year when a beautiful birthday cake was brought to the table with a frisky bunch of parsley waving from its middle.) I like the taste, texture, and color of fresh-chopped parsley and use it on vegetables, salads, omelets, potatoes, and soups. Summer or winter, I am never without it. It can be prepared by hand or blender, will keep three or four days in an open jar (lined with paper towel) on your work table, after which it will turn into unusually colorful, tasty dried parsley (a stage I seldom reach).

TO PREPARE PARSLEY BY HAND

On a wooden chopping board cut off stems from as much *unwashed* parsley as you wish to use. (Since there is good flavor in the stems, these can be added to soups, casseroles, etc.) Using a heavy knife, hold the tip down firmly on the chopping board with your left hand (as lever) and chop the parsley rapidly back and forth (in small semicircles) with your right hand until it is finely chopped. Rinse out a heavy clean dish-cloth in cold water, wring out, and pour parsley into the center of the cloth. Fold the corners to form a light bag and hold under running cold water, rinsing and squeezing a few times to clean the parsley. One last hard squeeze to eliminate every drop of water possible and then turn out contents of cloth on doubled paper towels. Spread thinly over the paper to dry, and leave for a few hours. Parsley will be bright green, soft, and fluffy. Store in open jar lined with paper towel.

BLENDER PARSLEY

Put parsley in a bowl of cold water and let stand for a few minutes. Drain and put in blender container until half full.

Cover with cold water until container is three quarters full. Turn motor on high speed for 5–6 seconds. Pour into a fine sieve and gently press out water with the back of a tablespoon. Turn parsley into a damp heavy dishcloth and squeeze hard. Turn out as above and store the same way.

FREEZER TIPS

Let your freezer work for you rather than vice versa. Cooking for the joy of squirreling away food can become an obsession. On the other hand, when baking, make extra pies, cakes, or cookies (which you can do with the minimum of effort and the maximum of later pleasure). Double or quadruple the recipes for casseroles and stews and freeze the excess. If I happen to be making crêpes, I make an extra fifty and freeze them unfilled; if I am buying unusual bread or other items that freeze well but are hard to come by, then I buy an extra quantity to stash away. I always have ice cream on hand because, combined with fruit (strawberries, peaches, etc., also frozen) or quickly made butterscotch* or chocolate sauce*, a popular party dessert is always at hand.

Chiefly, however, I use my freezer for leftovers. Egg whites (labeled as to number if you want to keep your sanity) can be frozen in small jars. Yolks must be beaten with 1 teaspoon salt per cup to freeze, but they seldom accumulate. If I have only one or two, I drop them into gently boiling water to hard-cook, and later they are grated over vegetables or salad. If there are several, they vanish into Hollandaise sauce, date bars, mayonnaise, etc. Whites turn into meringues, cookie glaze, cookies, and one or two added to a soufflé will make it soar. Other leftovers include stock, meat sauces, gravy, soups, cooked meat and poultry (especially chicken, which is fine for salad and sandwiches at short notice). Leftover heavy cream is whipped and frozen, which has a double advantage. Defrosted, it can be piped on to a dessert for glamour (if not quite stiff enough, beat for a minute or two) or it can be allowed to become liquid again and served with coffee.

It is my belief, backed by every expert I know, that fresh meat is juicier, tastier, and tenderer than frozen. The latter can be good, and sometimes tempting bargains make the compromise worthwhile. But to use frozen meat solely to avoid the bother of marketing seems almost wicked.

TO "REFRESH" GREEN VEGETABLES

When cooking green vegetables ahead (such as broccoli, asparagus, green beans), cook until barely tender and refresh. This means remove the vegetable from the heat, carefully transfer to a colander, and rinse under a gentle spray of *cold* water. This restores the color and, at the same time, stops the cooking. Let cool. When ready to reheat, put in pan with butter, fresh lemon juice, and herbs, and cook over medium heat.

BLENDERS

Next to diamonds, a blender can be a girl's best friend. Given a chance, it will do almost anything. It will chop nuts, pulverize crumbs, blend sauces, grind giblets, purée vegetables, beat salad dressings, enable you to improvise soups—all these and more besides. It is possible to get along without one, but much easier and pleasanter to cook with one at your elbow.

MIXERS

Mixers are wonderful, too, although not nearly so versatile as blenders. Cakes, cookies, fillings, frostings, salad dressings (such as vinaigrette sauce) can be produced with the minimum of effort. Nothing makes me feel more cosseted than to put eggs and sugar into the mixer, start the action, and move off for 10 minutes. On my return the ingredients have become thick and mousselike and require only flour, a dash of cinnamon, and a shove into the oven. All this inactivity produces a light, feathery, most delicious spongecake*. To scrape the blades— *scrape inside and out with a grapefruit knife.* Its curved surface easily removes the elusive batter, dough, or frosting.

ODDS AND ENDS

GARLIC

To mince garlic—peel cloves and put on wooden board. Salt heavily, and with the tip end of a sharp paring knife mash garlic and salt together until garlic is reduced to pulp.

GARLIC BUTTER

½ *pound butter at room temperature*
2 *cloves garlic, minced*
¼ *teaspoon lemon juice*

1 *tablespoon finely chopped parsley*
Salt to taste

Beat together butter and garlic until smooth. Add lemon juice and parsley. Season with salt. Keep covered in refrigerator.

To give salad dressing a lift—add peeled split clove of garlic to the jar. Remove in a day or two.

TO CONCASS TOMATOES

When tomatoes are scarce or the salad bowl requires only the addition of a little color, these make a fine decoration. To concass tomatoes—cut into quarters, unpeeled, and remove the insides (these can be added to soups, casseroles, etc.), leaving only the red shells. Cut these into narrow strips, trimming ends. One tomato furnishes a large quantity of these strips. Put them in the bottom of the salad bowl after tossing greens, and then scatter over finished salad, slaw, or cucumbers.

BUTTERED BREAD CRUMBS

1 cup bread crumbs   *1 tablespoon chopped*
4 tablespoons butter   *parsley*
                           Paprika

Sauté crumbs in hot butter until browned. Add parsley and paprika.

ONIONS

After peeling onions for boiling, make two crossed gashes on the root end. This will prevent them from disintegrating during cooking.

BUTTER AND FLOUR LIAISON

Knead equal parts butter and flour together with a fork until well blended and soft. To thicken a dish—rub liaison around sides of pan over heat and let dissolve into whatever is cooking.

MARINADE

The object of a marinade is to make meat more tender, moist, and well flavored. Less tender cuts of meat may be improved by marinating for many hours, while better cuts require less time. The usual time is from 4 to 24 hours, depending on the cut.

FOR BEEF

1 cup oil
½ cup red wine
2 cloves of garlic peeled
    and cut in two
4 shallots, or 1 small
    onion finely chopped

1 teaspoon salt
6 peppercorns
½ teaspoon basil
4 parsley sprigs

FOR LAMB

½ cup oil
¼ cup red wine
1 teaspoon salt
½ teaspoon orégano
1 clove of garlic peeled
    and cut in two

2 tablespoons mint leaves
    or 1 teaspoon dried finely
    chopped
3 parsley sprigs
6 peppercorns

Marinate at room temperature (unless doing so overnight).
Turn occasionally.

DRYING FRESH HERBS

Herbs for drying should be picked just before flowering.
Gather herbs on a dry day but not in the full sun. Tie in bundles
and hang up until dry and brittle. Or arrange on paper towels
covered by cheesecloth. When leaves are thoroughly dry, strip
them off the stalks and crush with fingers or rolling pin. Store
in airtight jars.

To dry parsley—wash and dry thoroughly, pick leaves from stalks, and lay on paper towels. Put in a warm place or in a slightly warm oven (heat must not exceed 125 degrees). Turn parsley over from time to time. If heat is constant, parsley will dry in a day or less. *Or dry parsley in a 375-degree oven for 1 minute.* The trick here is to avoid scorching, so watch carefully.

CARE AND TREATMENT OF COMMERCIALLY DRIED HERBS

Keep them in a closed cupboard away from sunlight. Check them from time to time and make sure when you buy them that they are a good green color. Brown overaged herbs taste like straw, so bravely toss out those that are no longer green.

MERINGUES

The success of meringues depends upon having the bowl and beaters absolutely dry and the egg whites at room temperature. It is safer to make them on a dry sunny day, and they will keep for days in an airtight tin covered with wax paper.

To soften meringues—put a piece of fresh bread in the tin for a few hours. Once I forgot meringues for several weeks, and this trick brought them back to chewy softness.

To crisp meringues—remove lid from cookie tin and expose them to the air. I find that in bad weather they sometimes get soft.

MISCELLANEOUS

When storing a dessert in the refrigerator (such as mousse, icebox cake, cheese cakes) line the shelf above with wax paper. This insures that nothing can drip down and cause damage.

To achieve best baking results—have your oven checked for accuracy at least twice a year. The best of stoves require correction from time to time, and it's an easy way to avoid disaster.

Preheat your oven in plenty of time before you are ready to use it. Let the oven wait for the cake instead of vice versa.

When using gelatin—always sprinkle it on the water or other dissolving liquid instead of vice versa.

Read a recipe all the way through before attempting to make a new dish. This has the double advantage of insuring that all ingredients are at hand and giving you a picture of the most efficient way to take each step.

IMPROVISE ! ! ! Trust your own judgment and taste buds. When first making a new recipe, follow instructions to the minutest detail, but after that add something of yourself. Make notes of your findings on each recipe card, giving the quantities used when adding extra or different herbs, flavoring, wine, or seasoning. Grow herbs if you possibly can—they can transform the simplest salad into an epicure's delight. Tackle anything and everything, and, sooner or later if you haven't already done so, you will discover that fine cooking is both creative and challenging and that hospitality, combined with good food, generates a welcome warmth in this tumultuous world.

INDEX